Improving Reading Comprehension and Speed, Skimming and Scanning, Reading for Pleasure

Second Edition

Marcia J. Coman · Kathy L. Heavers

NTC Publishing Group
a division of NTC/CONTEMPORARY PUBLISHING GROUP
Lincolnwood, Illinois USA

3 1450 00428 2356

Acknowledgments

Grateful acknowledgment is made to the following for permission to reprint copyrighted materials:

Employment & Training Administration, U.S. Employment Service, Washington, DC 20210, for "Merchandising Your Talents."

Kendall Slee, for "One Night in the Woods."

J. Weston Walch, Publisher, for excerpts from *Speedreading for Better Grades* by Ward Cramer. Copyright 1978 by J. Weston Walch, Publisher; Portland, Maine. Used with permission. All further reproduction prohibited.

J. Patrick Hooley, for "Creating Successful Study Habits."

Mary Lael Van Riper, for "Mary Had a Little Lamb."

Metra Commuter Rail, Chicago, Illinois, for excerpts from the Metra (Union Pacific/Northwest Line) timetable, 1996.

Fred Matheny, for "Cycling Risks" from *Beginning Bicycle Racing* by Fred Matheny, copyright 1983.

The Denver Post, for excerpts from selected sports and weather sections from *The Denver Post*, and *The Denver Post* Newspaper in Education Department, for excerpts from the 1994 *Colorado Career Guide*.

ISBN: 0-8442-5887-3

Published by NTC Publishing Group,
a division of NTC/Contemporary Publishing Group, Inc.,
4255 West Touhy Avenue,
Lincolnwood (Chicago), Illinois 60646-1975 U.S.A.
© 1998 NTC/Contemporary Publishing Group, Inc.
890 CU 098765432

Contents

Improving Your Understanding

You have just closed your book after reading an entire assignment that you thought you understood. But already your mind is blank, and you can't remember anything about what you read. Now you will have to spend more time rereading those pages or, worse still, the chapter.

If this situation is all too familiar, you'll be glad to hear that you can improve your comprehension. There are strategies to give you some "mental hooks" on which to hang the information that is vital to your success in school and life. Learning these comprehension survival skills will take effort, practice, and determination, but you cannot overlook them if you want to be a successful student.

To begin improving comprehension, first learn how to recognize main ideas. If you can identify the main ideas—and remember them—in the material you read, you have almost won the comprehension battle.

Finding the main idea may be difficult for two reasons: First, you may not know what a main idea is. The main idea is simply the point the author is trying to get across. It is the gist or substance of a paragraph; the thought that all the other details or pieces of information help support or illustrate. As you read, ask yourself, "What point is the author making in this paragraph?" The answer to your question is the author's main idea.

The second reason recognizing the main idea may be difficult is that you don't know where in the material to look for it. Is it in the first or last sentence, or is it sandwiched somewhere in the middle of the paragraph? Authors can place their paragraph's main idea anywhere. Look for it to come in the first sentence, a middle sentence, or the last sentence. Or, find it in the first sentence and see it restated in the last sentence, in a middle sentence or not stated at all! Think of finding the material's main idea as participating in a scavenger hunt; you know what kind of thing to look for, but not exactly where to find it. You'll have to actively search for it.

This unit will help you develop your ability to recognize main ideas. You will begin by selecting the key words in a sentence, then move on to identifying the main idea in a paragraph. Once you can do that, you will practice recognizing main ideas in longer works. Your goals, then, are:

1. to learn to identify key words in a sentence;
2. to learn to identify the main idea in a paragraph; and
3. to learn to identify the major points of a longer selection.

ACTIVITY 1.1

Recognizing Key Words in a Sentence

To find the main idea in a paragraph, you have to begin by recognizing key words in a sentence. Key words are the important or essential words—the words that determine the meaning of the sentence. Activity 1.1 will give you practice in picking out key words.

On a separate sheet of paper, number from one to ten, skipping every other line. Read the following sentences and list their key words on your paper. The first sentence is done as a sample.

1. You are to report to the principal's office immediately and take your books with you.
    Answer: You report principal's office immediately take books
2. The tryouts for the fall play will be this Thursday evening at 8:00 P.M. in Room 208.
3. The flood destroyed homes, bridges, and roads as it swept furiously through the canyon.
4. The Fourth of July is a special day in the United States because on that date the nation celebrates its independence.
5. Many states experience wide temperature changes during the four seasons.
6. Susan Smith and Joan Vickers ran for president of their class, and Joan won.
7. The football championship was a tie between North and South High Schools.
8. Peer pressure is often a problem for preteens and teens.
9. Regular attendance in school is important if you want to get good grades.
10. Concentration is required as you read these sentences if you wish to identify the key words.

ACTIVITY 1.2

Recognizing Main Ideas in a Paragraph

Once you have developed the ability to identify key words in a sentence, you will find it easier to pick out the main idea in a paragraph. Again, the main idea is the point the author is making; all other sentences in the paragraph work to support or develop this main idea.

On a separate sheet of paper, list the key or main idea in each of the following paragraphs. The first paragraph is done as a sample.

Paragraph One

Young people are faced with many decisions today. They have to choose between drinking or not drinking alcohol. They have to choose between smoking or not smoking. Some of them even choose between chewing tobacco or not chewing tobacco. For many, the decisions are difficult ones.
Answer: Young people are faced with many decisions today.

Paragraph Two

If it is sunny outside, do you feel cheerful? If it is rainy, do you feel depressed? Does the weather affect you? Hot weather makes some people irritable. Others complain that humid weather makes them tired.

Paragraph Three

Most schools are required to offer courses in English, math, science, social studies, and physical education. Schools also offer classes in art, industrial arts, computer science, music, foreign languages, agriculture, business, and auto mechanics. They provide opportunities before, during, and after school for sports, clubs, and other activities. Schools counsel students, reward students, correct students, and even feed students, in addition to educating them. Schools serve a variety of needs.

Paragraph Four

Students have many opportunities to become a part of a group and to acquire a sense of belonging. They can try out for sports teams or become a team manager. They can audition for a play or sing in a choir. They can participate on the speech team or be a member of the chess club. They can join a religious group or become a peer counselor. There are many ways to get involved.

Paragraph Five

We began the day by touring the Museum of Natural History. After we had lunch, we visited the Museum of Fine Arts and had snacks on the top floor terrace. Next, we went to the Planetarium and finished with dinner at a fancy downtown restaurant.

Paragraph Six

By now you know several things about the main idea of a paragraph. You know the main idea summarizes or expresses the major point being made in the paragraph. You know the main idea can be found at the beginning of a paragraph, at the end of a paragraph, within a paragraph, or at the beginning *and* end of a paragraph. You know most paragraphs have a main idea that is stated, but you also know that the main idea can be omitted and only implied. Finally, you know that finding the main idea in the paragraph is one of the first steps toward good comprehension.

ACTIVITY 1.3

Recognizing Main Ideas in an Article

Now work with an article that contains many paragraphs. Read "Use of Credit" and write down on a separate sheet of paper what you consider to be the main ideas of the article. As you read, remember to ask yourself the following: What points are the authors making in this selection?

Next, focus on the supporting details in the article. List the advantages and disadvantages of credit.

Use of Credit

Credit is one money management tool. It is considered a tool because it can be used to realize goals that you have decided to emphasize. Credit can expand buying power and simplify recordkeeping; however, if credit purchases are not related to income and payments are missed, the result is a poor credit history and financial worries. In some cases use of too much credit may lead to bankruptcy.

Credit use can be inexpensive or costly. Many credit grantors do not charge interest for credit card purchases when the balance is paid in full each month. Other types of credit, such as consumer loans, may add interest charges of 36 percent per year. You can decide which type fits your needs.

Consider both the advantages and disadvantages of using credit. As you think about the ways that credit plays a role in your money management program, you may decide to either expand or reduce your use of credit. Credit decisions are very individual and can have beneficial as well as disastrous consequences. This means that you will have to make a conscious decision about how to use credit.

Advantages.   Young people often have greater needs than current income. Credit may be the way to make large purchases such as a home, education, furniture, and appliances.

By borrowing to buy an item, people will have the use of it before they own it. A good example is an automobile—few people can afford to pay cash, and yet most people considered this an essential purchase.

Sometimes the only way to cope with an emergency is to borrow to pay expenses, especially when emergency medical care is needed or unemployment reduces income.

Credit can be used for investments. A house is important for shelter and in recent years has been an excellent investment. Most people usually do not have enough cash to buy a home without credit.

Credit allows people to enjoy conveniences today. Some families find washing clothes at home rather than at a laundromat a real time-saver. A loan may provide an opportunity to add a second bathroom to a home with a growing family.

Using a credit card while traveling can be a great convenience over carrying large amounts of money or trying to cash personal checks.

For people who find it difficult to save for purchases, credit payments may be considered a form of forced savings.

There are also tax advantages for borrowers. Mortgage interest is tax deductible for those who itemize expenses.

Disadvantages.   Consumers may overspend. One-third of all U.S. households have bank credit cards, and 70 percent of those who use cards generally pay only the minimum monthly payment. We have the tendency to spend more money when we charge items compared to paying cash. Researchers concerned with department store purchases found that the average cash sale was $8.25, the average store credit card purchase was $15.93, and the average bank card sale was $20.47. Many people have more than one bank card. When their line of credit on one card is used up, they switch to another card.

Credit has been relatively easy to get, and consumers have found themselves adding credit card to credit card and loan on top of loan to their outstanding debt.

People overlook the fact that when they buy an item they are paying twice for it, first for the item itself and second for the credit they use. Finance charges add to the price of goods and services. For example, we'll assume that a loan is for a travel trailer. The cost of the trailer is $5,000. The credit charges add an additional $902.32 to the price. Credit ties up future income, which means less flexibility for tomorrow's purchases.

Recognizing Sequence by Making Lists

If organization is a strong skill of yours, sequencing (placing things in order) may not seem difficult. If, on the other hand, you often ask yourself "What shall I do first?" or "Why are things so disorganized?" this group of exercises will help you begin thinking sequentially. Remembering becomes much easier when you can arrange the information you read in some sort of order, and catching on to the sequence will improve your comprehension skills as well. Your goal is to read and place things in your mind and memory in logical order.

Making Lists

Determine a heading for each of the following sentences. On a separate sheet of paper, write the heading and list the items in the sentence sequentially as they are presented. The first is done for you.

1. My grocery list included apples, flour, salt, and sugar.
   Answer: Groceries
   1. apples
   2. flour
   3. salt
   4. sugar

2. As he entered the room, he stopped with mouth wide open and eyes rounded in horror.

3. Mr. Smith presented two band awards this year: the Spirit Award and the prestigious John Phillip Sousa Award.

4. The following local scholarships are available to seniors: Columbine Honor Society, Elks, Altrusa, Frank-McKee Memorial, Lions Club, Music Teachers, and Rotary Club International.

5. As she looked forward to a new school year, Sue knew she would need to purchase a backpack, pens, pencils, paper, spiral notebooks, an eraser, and a highlighter.

ACTIVITY 1.5

Recognizing Sequence by Putting Steps in Order

Determining the order in which to do things requires comprehension or understanding. Try your hand at the following passage in which the steps are scrambled. Unscramble the steps and write them in the logical order on your paper.

How to Scramble Eggs

Pour in mixture and reduce heat to low. Heat ½ tablespoon fat for each egg in moderately hot skillet. Break eggs into bowl. When cooked through but still moist (5 to 8 minutes), serve at once. Add 1 tablespoon milk or cream and a dash of salt and pepper for each egg. Cook slowly, turning gently as mixture sets at bottom and sides of pan. Beat well with a fork. Avoid constant stirring.

ACTIVITY 1.6

Recognizing Sequence by Listing Procedures

Now try your skills on a longer selection. This time you will sequence procedures. Read the following questions so you know your purpose for reading the selection and the questions you should be answering as you read. Then read the selection. On a separate sheet of paper:

1. List the three time periods involved in a job interview. Leave space below each time period.

2. Under each time period, list the important points or tips for that portion of the interview.

3. Conclude by writing a brief paragraph summarizing the sequence of procedures in a job interview.

The Job Interview

Once you have an appointment for a job interview, there are certain things that should be done. These can basically be divided into three time periods—before, during, and after the interview.

Dress appropriately as you prepare for the interview. Wear clothes that are commonly worn or accepted in your interviewer's profession. If you are not sure what is appropriate to wear, ask for advice from others, or someone you know in that profession. Dress as if you could go to work at that location immediately.

Go to the interview alone and arrive five to ten minutes early. Being early shows that you are eager and responsible enough to be prompt. You must have done your homework, of course, and know what the company you hope to join makes or the services it provides.

Before leaving for the interview, be sure that you have your Social Security card, several copies of your résumé, and the names, addresses, and phone numbers of at least three people who are not relatives to be used as references or sources of information about you. If the job would include driving as part of the duties, take your driver's license, as well.

During the interview, be polite. Don't smoke or chew gum. Try to look as alert as possible, neither slouching nor sitting ramrod straight. Make frequent eye contact and listen intently to what the interviewer is saying. Answer his or her questions clearly and completely, speaking audibly. *Do not mumble*. Don't hesitate to ask questions of the interviewer as they occur to you, but wait to ask about benefits and vacations until you are actually offered the job. If you are not offered the job but want it, say so to the interviewer. Do not be demanding; simply state confidently that you would like to have the position.

After the interview, be sure to thank the interviewer for spending his or her time to talk with you. After the interview, write a thank you note. This is a polite gesture, often neglected, that may help the interviewer keep you in mind.

If you were told by the interviewer that he or she would contact you, and you do not get a response, call or make a return visit. Perseverance often wins jobs.

Understanding Character Development

ACTIVITY 1.7

You probably remember being asked to read a piece of literature and describe its main character. You were to discuss what the person was like at the beginning of the book and how that person changed. This kind of assignment also involves sequencing. Your purpose in reading required you to trace, in an orderly fashion from the beginning to the conclusion, the development of the main character.

Try that with the following paragraphs. On a separate sheet of paper, first list details that describe the new employee at the beginning of the story, then at the middle of the story, and finally at the end of the story. Then list, in the order they appeared or happened, the people and events that caused the main character to change.

At Last—The Job!

I had passed the test of the interview with flying colors, was given *the* job, and had started to work. Before, my experience had come chiefly from TV, movies, and my imagination. Unfortunately, mind games had not prepared me for the difficult period of adjustment that every inexperienced waitress must face: mixed-up orders, tired feet, spilled Coke, irate customers, crying babies, tired feet, littered tables, sticky plates, and tired feet—and all for small tips.

As you can imagine, I soon became so discouraged with myself and so dissatisfied with my job that I considered quitting. I think my supervisor must have felt the negative vibrations coming from my exhausted self, because she called me into her office and talked to me about both the duties of my new profession and the challenges they presented for sharpening my organizational skills to a fine edge. She also pointed out the direct relationship between my organizational abilities and service and the size of my tip.

That conversation with her helped me change my attitude considerably. I realized then that there was nothing wrong with me or my job that experience and a big smile could not cure. I decided to stay on.

ACTIVITY 1.8

Visualizing Character

As you improve your comprehension skills, you will gain a broader understanding of what you read. You also will remember more if you can train yourself to project mentally beyond the printed, literal meanings.

Think about the new employee in Activity 1.7. What kind of a visual image do you have of that person? Is that person a young girl or a middle-aged woman? How does she look, dress, and act? Through the course of the story, how does she change? Creating a vivid visual image of a character in your mind helps you remember the content of what you read.

Try it. As you read, create a visual image of the characters or scenes being presented in the following five descriptions. Draw from your own experiences and observations. Become that person! It's fun, and you will be surprised at how much longer and more vivid your memory of what you read will be.

On a separate sheet of paper, write a description of the character you "see" in each of the following sentences.

1. Long lashes lowered, she scuffed her patent leather shoes in the dust as she pulled at the ribbon that was her sash.

2. Always shabby in dress and committed to collecting aluminum cans, he never went out to lunch unless I was buying.

3. Massive in stature, his bellowing voice and swooping gestures, combined with his unkempt grey hair and grizzled beard, tended to put people off.

4. His changes of mood and wide-eyed whoops of laughter made his strange predictions very unsettling.

5. As the model pivoted on the runway, teeth flashing, tresses flying, and skirt swirling, I imagined a regal queen, accepting homage from loyal subjects.

Understanding Character Through Background

If you read about a character, visualizing and working to understand him or her based on details of the character's life, you have good comprehension of the character as a whole.

As you read the following paragraphs, try to visualize and then understand the great composer Johannes Brahms. Then, on a separate sheet of paper, answer these questions:

1. Why did Brahms never dare to get married?

2. Form an opinion or make a judgment regarding Brahms' character; justify your own view of it based on your understanding of the man.

Johannes Brahms, 1833–1897

Few great composers had more difficult early years than Brahms. When Brahms was in his teens, he would perform in the waterfront saloons to earn money for his family. Even then, Brahms never used sheet music, for he could play everything from memory.

When he was twenty, Brahms was introduced by letter to the noted composer Robert Schumann. Schumann and his wife, Clara, took Brahms and his music to their hearts. When it became necessary for Schumann to enter an asylum for the insane, Brahms comforted Clara and gradually fell in love with her. Even after Schumann died, two years later, Brahms never spoke of marriage. (He was known for becoming very close to several women, only to bow out of the relationship.) Brahms once said that there were two things he had never dared to try: opera and marriage.

Brahms spent the last half of his life in Vienna, a noted city of music. He was seen as a privately generous, publicly crusty, boorish bachelor. He lived in the simplest of rooms and rose every morning at five o'clock. With his baggy, unimpressive appearance, bulky form, high voice, and his shovel-shaped beard, he was a familiar figure. Those that knew him loved that part of him which was forever young.

This rather disheveled, outwardly eccentric man, who kept his money tied up in bundles and got some of his best ideas while shining his shoes, was one of the supreme architects of complex, orderly musical structure—the symphony.

Sensing Relationships Between Cause and Effect

As your comprehension skills grow sharper, you will soon realize that many of your classes deal, very basically, with what happened first and second and then third to cause an end result. Think of studying the Civil War, for example. You begin by looking at the causes of the war, then the war itself, and finally the effects of the war on the United States and even the world.

Sometimes events are not clearly spelled out in a simple first-second-third sequence, however, and you must dig to uncover information. If you have to make a search, it is helpful to first clearly identify what happened (the cause). Then use your skills at locating key thoughts and proper sequence to uncover the clues necessary to find the target result (or the effect).

Practice identifying reading clues and targets, and your comprehension skills will improve even more because you are alert as you read, actively searching for answers. Your reading rate will improve because you know exactly what you are looking for.

Consider the following example. Jeff has gotten a poor grade on a test because he didn't study, but instead of accepting the grade, he begins arguing with his instructor in an attempt to get more points. After several unsuccessful attempts on Jeff's part, the instructor firmly responds, "Jeff, that's enough!" Jeff is silent.

By following the sequence and reading between the lines, what does this example say to you? The content reveals exactly what Jeff has done and how his instructor responded. But beyond that, what else do you know?"

Jeff was silent. What did Jeff anticipate?

What can you point to as the cause of the instructor's response?

How would you describe the instructor's mood?

What would you anticipate would happen if Jeff continued to argue?

You can see that the answers to these questions are not printed in the paragraph above. To come up with the answers, you have to think beyond what is printed. And to do that, you use higher-level thinking skills.

Concentrate on the sequence of events as you read the following paragraphs. After you finish reading, consider the relationships that are established between the causes and the effects to answer the questions that follow each paragraph. Write your answers on a separate sheet of paper.

Paragraph One

It is a beautiful, sunny summer day, and Tony and Roberto decide to go fishing. Tony grabs he fishing poles and a net, Roberto packs a quick lunch, and they set off. When they reach the lake, they discover they are missing an important item for their fishing excursion.

1. What are Tony and Roberto missing?
2. What will be the effect of fishing without this item?
3. Conversely, if they catch no fish, what is the cause?

Paragraph Two

Yoshimi has gone to the store to buy a birthday present for her mother. She has ten dollars that her father gave her along with specific instructions as to what to purchase. She is to buy a necklace her mother has been hinting about for weeks. As she passes by the store window, Yoshimi sees a purse that she just *has to* have. The purse is on sale for five dollars, and she buys it, She buys her mother a small pair of earrings with the remaining money.

1. What will Yoshimi's father's reaction be?
2. What is the cause of his reaction?
3. What will Yoshimi's mother's reaction be?
4. What is the cause of her reaction?
5. How will her parents' reactions affect Yoshimi?

Paragraph Three

Sean has a part-time job after school at a small grocery store. It is his responsibility to gather the grocery carts from the parking lot and bring them indoors. After the first month of work, he arrives on Tuesday twenty minutes late; his boss comments on it. The following Tuesday he arrives twenty minutes late again; his boss warns him about being late. Again, the next Tuesday, Sean arrives twenty minutes late. His boss is in the parking lot gathering the grocery carts himself.

1. What do you anticipate Sean's boss will do?
2. What are the causes of his boss's actions?
3. Is this result fair for Sean?

Analyzing Causes and Their Effects

Sometimes, causes and their effects are not obvious as you read . To understand the material, you may need to *analyze* it. For example, if you fail a test, you need to analyze the causes of your failing in order to avoid failing again. Once you determine why your test answers were incorrect, you can avoid repeating the same kinds of mistakes on a second test. You analyze the cause of making mistakes to avoid their effect—failure of another test.

Activity 1.11 will give you practice in analyzing causes and their effects. Read "Good Listening Is Difficult" and, on a separate sheet of paper, list seven reasons (or causes) for difficulty in listening. Conclude by explaining what the effect of poor listening skills might be on grades.

Good Listening Is Difficult

Many students would agree that listening is a difficult skill. For most, it is much harder to master new material by listening to a lecturer than by reading a textbook. Since listening, like reading, is a popular method of teaching, both in and out of school, it is important to understand why listening well is so difficult.

When listening, you have to adjust to the speed of speakers. If they speak very rapidly, you may not be able to take in all that they say. On the other hand, if they are very slow and deliberate, you may find it hard to keep your mind on what they are saying. (Your mind's pace is much more rapid than that of *any* speaker.)

You may not be mentally prepared for listening. You may not know anything about the topic and may be confused until you have heard enough to understand and focus on the subject being considered. Perhaps you don't feel well, or you are caught up in a daydream. You cannot choose the time and place for listening.

Unfortunately, there is no "replay button" to push when you are listening. If you miss what was said the first time, it is gone. You have missed it.

It is hard to be a listener and a critical thinker at the same time. When you are reading and you want to stop and consider a particular point, you can put the book aside and do so. However, when you are listening, such lengthy evaluations are not possible.

Distractions are all around you—particularly in the classroom. You may sit by a window and have a tendency to look out and watch the world. Maybe the person behind you has news about something in which you are very interested. Perhaps you would like to date the person seated across the aisle. Once your attention wanders from the speaker, it is hard to concentrate again.

Personal biases or prejudices may make it difficult for you to keep an open mind. Speaking style or physical appearance may influence the way you respond to what you hear. Listening with understanding and reserving judgment until later is difficult for most people.

The reaction of others to a topic or speaker may influence your ability to make a judgment about what the speaker is saying. Weighing the evidence and mentally keeping up with what the speaker is really saying is challenging when others have prejudged and are urging agreement.

Nevertheless, in spite of some of the roadblocks you have just read about, efficient listening in class is a skill that anyone who is committed to becoming a better listener can learn.

ACTIVITY 1.12   Recognizing Inferences and Drawing Conclusions

Are you a good detective? Sometimes you need to be, to understand a situation, make inferences, and draw conclusions from what you read when the results are not clearly stated.

To make inferences, you have to go beyond given words or circumstances to draw conclusions. For example, suppose you just bought a new red pen, and you are certain you left it on your desk. But the pen in missing. You find a note written in red ink by your brother. What do you infer, or what conclusions do you draw, based on your understanding of the situation?

Identifying main ideas, noting the sequence of events, visualizing the material clearly, and targeting the outcome are all skills that you have been acquiring. Now, put them to work and have some fun practicing your sleuthing as you complete the following exercises. Your goals are to understand, to make inferences, and to draw conclusions from what you read.

Begin by reading the following sentences. Then, on a separate sheet of paper, explain what conclusions you have drawn, or predict what might, will, or has happened, based on your understanding of the facts given. The first sentence has been done for you as an example.

1. Take your umbrella, as the clouds look very threatening off to the west.

   Conclusion or prediction: It might rain.

2. Yelling and booing and pointing at the referee followed the final call.

3. It's snowing, blowing, and about two degrees above zero outside.

4. The strange creature was covered with feathers, had a long, sharp bill, and gave shrill, raucous cries when approached by onlookers.

5. The tree was decorated, the stockings were hung, and the smell of pies baking wafted through the house.

6. The three contestants stood in a row, each nervously awaiting the spin of the wheel.

7. In spite of the deafening roar of the fans, the eleven helmeted men lined up, the referee blew the whistle, and the ball was kicked into the air.

8. The student held his breath as his paper was handed back. A quick glance at the top brought a grim expression.

9. A beaker, a few chemicals, and a loud BANG. They had done it again.

10. The hastily drawn posters were hung on the walls, the speeches were nervously given, and the votes were finally tallied. Jana smiled broadly.

Cloze

Another activity that focuses on improving your comprehension is cloze. The word *cloze* comes from the term *closure* and means to bring completion to a sentence. A cloze activity is a puzzle of sorts; you use the clues provided in the context to think of appropriate words to fill the blanks. The purpose of cloze is to teach you to use context clues to figure out the meanings of words you don't know. Cloze improves your reading comprehension, as well.

Read the following selection through first, mentally supplying the words you think belong in the spaces. Then, on a separate sheet of paper, number from one to thirty-two. Read "One Night in the Woods" again, filling in each blank with a word from the list provided. All the words in the list must be used, and some words will be used more than once. Finish by writing the word beside the appropriate number on your paper.

popped	first	five	at	was
fresh	prickles	had	the	imaginations
you	especially	hill	crept	trails
stage	or	moon	tried	a
shadows	feet	imaginary	and	enough
does	I	not	mountainside	

One Night in the Woods

The fresh pine scent in the air made me glad to be out of the stuffy cabin and away from my sleeping companions. I had no flashlight, but it ____1____ just a short way up the ____2____ to the other cabin, and the ____3____ was shining. Confidently I started up ____4____ trail.

Soon I realized that it ____5____ not as bright as I had ____6____ thought. The moon slyly cast only ____7____ light to create eerie shadows. The ____8____ air rattled the aspen leaves. It ____9____ not the chilly air that caused ____10____ to crawl down my spine.

Do ____11____ know Jason? He has retired from ____12____ movie *Friday the 13th* into the ____13____ of many. Now he slithered into my thoughts. Do you know what Jason ____14____ ? He murders people walking up mountain ____15____ in the middle of the night, ____16____ when they're alone.

The moon ____17____ no mercy. It kept the eerie ____18____ set. "Shuuushsh," said something in the ____19____. Was it the shadow that moved ____20____ something *in* it? I shuddered and ____21____ to control my frightened thoughts.

After ____22____ more careful steps, I plainly heard ____23____ twig snap behind me. *Is Jason ____24____ ?* I instantly felt my heart pounding ____25____ my ribs in panic. Silent horror ____26____ to every part of my body. ____27____ could not look back. With heavy ____28____ I plodded forward.

When another twig ____29____ behind me, I froze. I was ____30____ imagining.

"BOO!" I jumped straight up ____31____ screamed. My terror resounded over the ____32____ . Amy's eyes filled with tears of merriment as she exploded into giggles. After a pause I, too, began to laugh.

On a separate sheet of paper, answer the following questions:

I. Completion

Number from one to five. Fill the blank with the term(s) from this unit that complete the statement.

1. The point the author is trying to get across is called the _____.

2. _____ is understanding the point the author is making.

3. Putting things in order is called _____. You must have a basic understanding in order to do this.

4. Comprehension involves understanding the basic relationship between _____ and effect.

5. _____ comes from the word *closure* and means to complete something. You need comprehension to bring appropriate closure to a sentence.

II. Short Essay

Read the following paragraphs. On a separate sheet of paper, write the number IIA and, below it, write IIB. Beside IIA write the main idea of the paragraphs. Beside IIB, list sequentially six things you can do to develop your skills as a student.

You Can Become a Better Student

There are several things you can do to become a better student. First, you can create a good study setting for yourself; where you study helps improve your concentration and comprehension.

Second, you can budget your time. Decide what subjects you need to study and in what order you should study them. Approximate how long each subject will take to study, time for breaks, and block out that amount of time in your schedule for the day.

Third, work on improving your note-taking abilities. Practice getting the main ideas down in as concise a manner as possible. Use abbreviations, personal shorthand, and a highlighter to mark the important points.

Next, develop and use good test-taking skills. Know the tricks for taking tests in general, as well as those suited to specific types of tests. Know how to handle test anxiety, how to budget your time when taking tests, and how to evaluate your test when it is returned, so that you can do better on the next test.

Fifth, understand the value of reading different material at appropriate and vastly different rates. Know when to speed up and when to slow down; know when to read at 100 words per minute and when to read at 1,000 words per minute. Then use those varying rates.

Finally, develop your listening skills. Sit away from friends, doors, windows, and other distractions. Don't prejudge speakers. Adjust to their speaking speed. And be an active listener; don't put your mind in neutral, but instead participate mentally in what the speaker is saying. Stay with that person—think about what he or she is saying.

Clearly, there are many things you can do to become a better student. Practice these techniques, and watch your grades improve.

III. Application

Choose *one* of the following (a *or* b).

a. Discuss in a brief paragraph some of the *causes* of poor grades and the *effects* poor grades may have on a student's life. Show by your discussion that you understand the cause-effect relationship.

b. Develop four inferences and demonstrate your understanding of the inferences by predicting an outcome or drawing a conclusion.

Example: Hour after hour, day after day, Luis pored over piles of notes, reviewed pages and pages in the text, and created sample test after sample test. He had to pass that final.
Prediction: Luis will pass the test because of all his preparation.

IV. Cloze

Read the entire selection, mentally selecting the appropriate word for the blank *as* you read. Next, number from one to twenty-four. Read "Planning Your Time" again, filling in the blanks with the words from the list provided. All words in the list must be used, and some words will be used more than once. Write the appropriate word in the correct space on your answer sheet.

lower	pays	time	or	your
employer	project	the	search	find
last	sight	should	for	take
in	are	as	of	

Planning Your Time

Even if you are under no economic pressure to find a job quickly, starting your search promptly is a wise policy. Delays may hurt your chances of finding the job you want. If you have just finished school, for example, you ___1___ competing for similar positions with other new graduates in ___2___ field. Moreover, a long delay between school or your ___3___ job and your application for work may give an ___4___ the impression that his or her office is one ___5___ your last stops in a long fruitless job ___6___ .

Once you start your search, you should treat it ___7___ a full-time job. Set realistic goals and keep ___8___ of them. It is important to remember that looking

____9____ work can be discouraging. Do not let employer rejections ____10____ your self-esteem or serve as an excuse to "____11____ a vacation" from job seeking. Sustained effort usually ____12____ off.

The following suggestions may help you plan your ____13____ for an efficient job search:

1. Plan and start your ____14____ as soon as you know you will need to ____15____ a new job.

2. Make your job hunting a full-time ____16____. You work a 40-hour week for your employer; you ____17____ work no less for yourself.

3. Once you start your ____18____, do not allow yourself little vacations.

4. Apply early enough ____19____ the day to allow time for multiple interviewers, tests, ____20____ other hiring procedures that may be required.

5. Be on ____21____ for appointments.

6. Before approaching a firm, try to learn ____22____ best time and day of the week to apply ____23____ a job.

7. Follow up leads immediately. If you learn ____24____ a job opening late in the day, call the firm to arrange an appointment for the next day. The employer may postpone a hiring decision until then.

Increasing Speed

Are you reading as well or as fast as you might? If not, don't despair—you are not alone! Most students receive no formal training in the "how to's" of reading after grade school. It is not surprising, then, that you may feel your skills don't meet the demands now being made on them.

Some students read everything at the same slow rate in order the maximize understanding of what they read. But problems come when reading speed is slow enough to allow daydreaming.

Whatever your reading rates, remember that speed and comprehension go hand in hand. Read slowly, and daydreaming sets in; read too fast, and little or nothing stays in your memory.

The information and exercises in Unit 2 will help you improve your reading speed—an area many students find to be a problem, no matter what the subject matter. If you are determined, and if you can exercise self-discipline, you can eliminate some inefficient reading habits that impede your success.

Reading rates are very personal. It is not important to compare your speed with that of another. What is important is that you are reading faster, comprehending more, and remembering longer. The final payoff will be in better understanding of the material and improved grades.

Rapid Discrimination Drills

Reading at a speed that is too slow leads to boredom and daydreaming because your brain is not challenged. If you find yourself daydreaming as you read, perhaps you need to try reading faster. Use the rapid discrimination drills in Activities 2.1 through 2.10 to push yourself to read more quickly.

The drills help you increase your reading speed because they force you to look at words and pick out, at very rapid rates, those that are alike or different. The drills train you to recognize word meanings quickly. In addition, they challenge you to take in longer and longer words at the same rapid rate in which you recognize the shorter words. To use the drills, follow this procedure:

1. Label the upper right-hand corner of a separate sheet of paper as shown:

	Min.	Sec.
Time stopped	_____	_____
Time began	_____	_____
Total time read	_____	_____

2. Number your paper from one to twenty.

If your instructor is timing the drill:

3. Listen carefully to instructions and do not begin working until your instructor gives you the signal.

4. Look up when you finish and record the total time you read based on the time card being held up by your instructor.

5. Correct your paper as your instructor gives the answers, and record the total time you read and your score on the chart you construct. (See the model chart at the end of this introduction.)

If your instructor is not timing the drill, use the following procedure:

3. Using a watch or clock with a second hand, note the time you begin on your sheet of paper.

4. Turn to the proper page, read the instructions at the top of that page, and complete the drill as quickly as possible.

5. Note the time you finish. Subtract the time you began from the time you finish to determine the total time you read. Grade your paper using the answer key in the appendix at the end of this unit. Then, compute your score by giving yourself five points for each correct answer; record your score on a chart such as the one shown below.

Remember, your goal is to improve or maintain your reading time and score while increasing the length of the words you are reading. To benefit more from these drills, practice them on four consecutive days, using three sequential exercises each day.

RAPID DISCRIMINATION DRILLS

		1	2	3	4	5	6	7	8	9	10
Different Word	Time										
	Score										
Same Word	Time										
	Score										
Meaning	Time										
	Score										

Rapid Discrimination Drill 1

ACTIVITY 2.1

Write the number of the word that is different.

	1	2	3	4	5
1.	site	site	site	side	site
2.	cord	cord	cord	cord	card
3.	nail	mail	nail	nail	nail
4.	maps	maps	naps	maps	maps
5.	pore	pore	pore	pore	bore
6.	raid	paid	paid	paid	paid
7.	look	look	book	look	look
8.	cake	rake	rake	rake	rake
9.	pear	tear	pear	pear	pear
10.	cook	cook	cook	took	cook
11.	felt	felt	felt	felt	melt
12.	cape	cape	tape	cape	cape
13.	jack	rack	rack	rack	rack
14.	veil	veil	veil	veal	veil
15.	hats	rats	hats	hats	hats
16.	jump	jump	jump	jump	pump
17.	pale	pale	dale	pale	pale
18.	pool	pool	pool	poor	pool
19.	tool	took	took	took	took
20.	cart	part	cart	cart	cart

Rapid Discrimination Drill 2

A key word is given. Write the column number in which it is repeated.

Key Word	1	2	3	4	5
1. dull	mull	pull	full	dull	cull
2. desk	mask	deck	pest	desk	risk
3. last	mast	last	past	task	fast
4. mask	mope	task	mask	make	made
5. made	raid	fade	paid	jade	made
6. rail	mail	tail	sail	rail	pail
7. hook	hook	took	book	look	cook
8. rule	mule	rule	tool	fool	cool
9. hope	rope	Pope	lope	nope	hope
10. took	took	cook	look	rook	book
11. bone	tone	moan	hone	bone	loan
12. clad	paid	made	fade	glad	clad
13. dirt	curt	tart	dirt	mart	bard
14. feel	meal	zeal	real	feel	peal
15. boat	moat	boat	coat	tote	goat
16. jeer	mere	fear	jeer	tear	leer
17. pony	pony	home	bone	tone	zone
18. real	peal	meal	teal	real	seal
19. pare	bare	mare	tare	fare	pare
20. belt	belt	felt	melt	pelt	welt

Rapid Discrimination Drill 3

List the number of the word(s) that mean(s) the same as the **key word**.

Key Word	1	2	3	4
1. site	hill	scene	place	land
2. spry	old	smart	active	thin
3. rely	ask	depend	expect	balk
4. balk	trip	fall	stop short	frighten
5. bask	play	sun	warm oneself	fry
6. vows	wish	promises	order	command
7. clue	hint	reminder	thought	answer
8. ajar	wide open	unlocked	closed	partly open
9. burr	rough edge	haircut	dig deep	sandy shore
10. hint	answer	slight sign	explanation	essay

11.	vary	shrink	increase	grow	change
12.	feat	foolish	skillful act	trip	flight
13.	chat	speech	easy talk	explanation	lecture
14.	chef	cook	dean	president	policeman
15.	clad	completely	appearing	dressed	working
16.	poll	campaign	question	debate	vote
17.	pant	behave	slight	short breath	enough
18.	odor	neither	smell	danger	taste
19.	rein	rain	reign	bridle strap	razor
20.	heir	session	who inherits	hair	ancestor

Rapid Discrimination Drill 4

Write the number of the word that is different.

	1	2	3	4	5
1.	blurt	flirt	flirt	flirt	flirt
2.	power	power	flour	power	power
3.	medal	metal	medal	medal	medal
4.	align	align	align	alien	align
5.	check	check	check	check	cheek
6.	burly	curly	burly	burly	burly
7.	abide	chide	chide	chide	chide
8.	flood	flood	flood	flood	blood
9.	trunk	trunk	trunk	chunk	trunk
10.	plush	plush	blush	plush	plush
11.	glaze	craze	craze	craze	craze
12.	twist	twist	twist	twist	wrist
13.	float	float	floor	float	float
14.	shade	shade	shade	shape	shade
15.	widow	width	widow	widow	widow
16.	hazy	hazy	crazy	hazy	hazy
17.	blush	plush	plush	plush	plush
18.	pedal	pedal	pedal	medal	pedal
19.	chase	chute	chase	chase	chase
20.	shame	shame	shame	shame	share

Rapid Discrimination Drill 5

A **key word** is given. Write the number of the column in which it is repeated.

Key Word	1	2	3	4	5
1. bonus	tones	bonus	cones	hones	phone
2. shame	share	shout	shoot	shore	shame
3. write	trite	sight	write	fight	white
4. weigh	weigh	worry	neigh	wrist	wring
5. glass	glare	globe	glaze	glass	gland
6. blunt	blunt	bloom	bloat	blown	black
7. dingy	diner	dingy	dings	dinky	dingo
8. wield	yield	field	wield	weird	waist
9. gland	gloom	glove	glory	glass	gland
10. wrist	twist	crust	wisps	wrist	grist
11. block	blare	block	blast	blank	blame
12. false	fable	faint	famed	false	fancy
13. boils	boils	toils	foils	coils	bowls
14. aides	maids	raids	aides	paids	fades
15. chase	chaff	chair	chain	chalk	chase
16. legal	legal	leach	leafy	leaky	learn
17. rebel	ready	rebel	realm	recur	reign
18. champ	chalk	chair	champ	chain	chaff
19. agent	again	agaze	agent	agile	aging
20. brief	brick	bribe	bride	brief	briar

Rapid Discrimination Drill 6

List the number of the word(s) that mean(s) the same as the **key word**.

Key Word	1	2	3	4
1. vocal	of voice	simple	harmonizing	loud
2. drawl	slow talk	fast talk	quiet talk	loud talk
3. elude	hide from	void	evade	discover
4. array	table	menu	amount	display
5. scent	choke	odor	sent	mail
6. sheer	very thin	shore	clean	cut
7. adapt	to learn	to modify	to probe	to notify
8. tempt	tame	test	threaten	trust
9. realm	flavor	kingdom	pilot	reality
10. agony	uncertain	pain	acute	scholar

11.	amuse	entertain	harp	ignorance	abuse
12.	alter	additional	graduate	altar	change
13.	prong	sharp edge	blade	pointed end	pin
14.	valet	housekeeper	cook	gardener	servant
15.	abode	dwelling	atmosphere	situation	surrounding
16.	foyer	basement	office	porch	entry hall
17.	horde	swarm	trace	rodent	family
18.	solar	of planets	of stars	of sun	of universe
19.	wield	lift up	accomplish	obtain	hold and use
20.	vivid	empty	cold	alive	dull blue

Rapid Discrimination Drill 7

Write the number of the word that is different.

	1	2	3	4	5
1.	belong	belief	belong	belong	belong
2.	census	census	census	censor	census
3.	facing	facing	facial	facing	facing
4.	agency	agenda	agenda	agenda	agenda
5.	device	device	device	device	devise
6.	tender	hinder	tender	tender	tender
7.	liking	liking	liking	likely	liking
8.	pardon	parent	parent	parent	parent
9.	jacket	jacket	racket	jacket	jacket
10.	triple	triple	triple	triple	ripple
11.	shrewd	shreds	shreds	shreds	shreds
12.	thresh	thresh	thrash	thresh	thresh
13.	reboil	recoil	reboil	reboil	reboil
14.	series	series	serial	series	series
15.	reform	reform	reform	reflex	reform
16.	snatch	snitch	snitch	snitch	snitch
17.	status	status	status	status	static
18.	gratis	gravel	gratis	gratis	gratis
19.	hooded	hooded	hooves	hooded	hooded
20.	tingle	tingle	tingle	mingle	tingle

Rapid Discrimination Drill 8

A **key word** is given. Write the number of the column in which it is repeated.

Key Word	1	2	3	4	5
1. modify	module	modest	modify	modern	models
2. nibble	pebble	treble	nimble	normal	nibble
3. pellet	pellet	mallet	ballet	market	target
4. rescue	resale	resume	resort	rescue	resist
5. sadden	saddle	sadden	sadder	sadism	sacred
6. spider	spinet	spinal	spiral	spider	spirit
7. broken	broken	broach	broker	bronze	brooms
8. change	chance	cancel	change	chapel	charge
9. commit	combat	comely	comets	common	commit
10. damper	damsel	damper	dampen	damask	damage
11. gamble	gander	gamble	gargle	garlic	garret
12. indent	indeed	indebt	indict	indent	indoor
13. jangle	jangle	jingle	jargon	jaunty	jersey
14. misuse	miscue	misery	misuse	misfit	mishap
15. oppose	option	oracle	orbits	orphan	oppose
16. radial	radios	radial	radium	radius	random
17. seaman	season	seater	secede	seaman	second
18. hubbub	hubbub	hugged	humble	humans	hunger
19. limber	linger	lining	limber	liquid	listen
20. memory	method	mental	midget	member	memory

Rapid Discrimination Drill 9

List the number of the word(s) that mean(s) the same as the **key word**.

Key Word	1	2	3	4
1. rustic	rural	rusty	normal	simple
2. hectic	dramatic	dull	very busy	angry
3. deluge	sprinkle	shower	heavy rain	fog
4. relish	care	speed	amusement	enjoy
5. defect	stowaway	noise	fault	repair
6. sultry	hot and humid	sunny	overcast	smelly
7. relent	soften	lend	surrender	hold firm
8. smudge	would	expression	dirt	smear
9. caress	lick	stroke	protect	warm
10. heroic	strong	loyal	friendly	brave

11.	tremor	loud noise	shaking	shock	frighten
12.	stench	stretch	dirty	stingy	bad smell
13.	differ	be like	be unlike	be kind	be common
14.	decree	infant	circular	rejoice	royal law
15.	hatred	flush	great dislike	hurt	sacred
16.	bestow	best one	give	take	put away
17.	offend	kettle	ladder	often	make angry
18.	define	settler	legal	state meaning	defend
19.	emerge	lead on	come out	dispute	image
20.	induce	bring about	enclose	sight	intrude

Rapid Discrimination Drill 10

Write the number of the word that is different.

	1	2	3	4	5
1.	baggage	bagpipe	bagpipe	bagpipe	bagpipe
2.	calcify	calcify	calcium	calcify	calcify
3.	dogwood	dolphin	dogwood	dogwood	dogwood
4.	flatcar	flatcar	flatcar	flatcar	flatten
5.	grating	grating	grating	gratify	grating
6.	hemline	hemlock	hemline	hemline	hemline
7.	illegal	illicit	illicit	illicit	illicit
8.	inverse	inverse	invalid	inverse	inverse
9.	justify	justify	justify	justify	justice
10.	kinetic	kinetic	kinetic	kindred	kinetic
11.	lapsing	larceny	lapsing	lapsing	lapsing
12.	martial	marshal	marshal	marshal	marshal
13.	nitrite	nitrite	nitrate	nitrite	nitrite
14.	offices	offices	offices	offices	officer
15.	plastic	plastic	plastic	plaster	plastic
16.	rampage	rampage	rampage	rampant	rampage
17.	recruit	rectify	recruit	recruit	recruit
18.	secular	section	section	section	section
19.	spastic	spastic	sparkle	spastic	spastic
20.	tipster	tipster	tipster	tipster	timeout

Timed Readings

We are creatures of habit, and it is easy to fall into the pattern of reading everything at the most comfortable rate. However, that is not an efficient way to read. Instead, you should vary your rate to suit your purpose, the difficulty of the material, and your background. Sometimes this means reading, without sacrificing comprehension, as quickly as you can. Of course, learning to read more rapidly takes practice, as does anything at which you want to improve.

One easy way to increase reading speed is to read a lot. Choose the type of material that interests you. In order to focus your attention on improving your reading speed, try this method of timed readings two or three times per week over a period of weeks.

1. Write the following on a separate sheet of paper.

number of lines read	(1)
× number of words per line	(2)
total number of words read	(3)
total number of words read	(4)
÷ number of minutes read	(5)
rate in words per minute	(6)

2. Select an article or chapter that interests you.

3. Before starting to read, determine the average number of words per line in the selection you have chosen. To do this, count all the words in 10 lines and divide by 10 for the average number of words per line. Write this number on your sheet of paper in Space 2.

    Number of words in 10 lines ÷ by 10 = average number of words per line

    If your instructor is timing, you will be told when to begin reading and when to stop.
    If your instructor is not timing, you will need a watch with a second hand or a timer.

4. Do two timed readings whenever you practice. Read each time for the same number of minutes. (We suggest three to six minutes per reading.)

5. Set a timer and begin reading at a comfortable rate. When the timer signals that your reading time is finished, note on your paper in Space 5 the number of minutes you read. Then mark your place in the material you read.

6. Count the number of lines you read and write this down in Space 1.

7. Figure the number of words per minute you read by multiplying the total number of lines (Space 1) by the average number of words per line (Space 2).

8. Column Two: Divide the total number of words you read (Space 3 or 4) by the number of minutes you read (Space 5). This figure will be the number of words per minute (wpm) that you read (Space 6).

Example:

1.	number of lines read	100
2.	number of words per line	× 6
3.	total number of words read	600
4.	total number of words read	600
5.	number of minutes read	÷ 3
6.	rate in words per minute	200

For your second timed reading, continue from where you finished before, pushing yourself to read as quickly as you can without losing comprehension. (This may seem awkward at first.) When you time is up, again compute your words read per minute using the same formula as before.

Record both your comfortable rate and your "push" rate on a chart you make on a separate sheet of paper. Use the following chart as an example.

SPEED-READING CHART

Date	Number of words/line	Number of lines	Number of minutes	Rate in words per minute
9/21	6	100	3	200

As you continue with your timed reading practices during class, you will see progress if you are serious about wanting to read faster. Be sure to compare the differences between your comfortable rates and your push rates, as well as noting your increases in reading speed.

Additional Activities to Increase Reading Speed[1]

There are several other activities you can do to improve your reading speed. You will need light, easy, and enjoyable reading material; choose something you look forward to reading. Make up your mind that you will push yourself beyond your normal reading rate; you will be surprised at how soon the new reading speed becomes comfortable for you.

Decide how much time you can spend on an activity and then select a drill from the suggestions that follow.

---

[1] The activities offered to increase reading speed are from *Improving Reading in Every Class* by Ellen Lamar Thomas and H. Alan Robinson, and *Reading Aids for Every Class* by Ellen Lamar Thomas. Both books were published by Allyn & Bacon, Inc., Boston.

One-Minute Speed Drills

This drill resembles the timed readings discussed previously. Read for one minute, determine your rate in words per minute, and record it on your Speed-Reading Chart. Then read for another minute, trying to beat your previous score. Do this for ten minutes several times a week.

One-Page Speed Drills

In this drill you read one page at a time and work for improvement. Note the time before you begin reading, read the page, and note the time upon ending reading. Try another one-page reading in an attempt to improve your previous time. Repeat this process two or three times a week.

Ten-Page Speed Drills

Count out ten pages and mark the tenth page with a paper clip, Note the time and begin reading. Push yourself. At the end of the tenth page, note the time again and determine how many minutes you spent reading. Record this time; it is this time you want to improve when you repeat the exercise with ten other pages.

One-Hour Speed Drills

Note the time and read for one hour. Count the number of pages you read. Your goal is to read more pages the next time you read for an hour using similar material.

One-Book Speed Drills

This drill is for avid readers. Determine the number of hours it takes you to read a book (approximately). Then divide the number of pages in a book you wish to read by the number of hours it usually takes you to finish reading.

Example: 200 pages in 4 hours = 50 pages per hour

Put a paper clip on the page you should reach after one hour of reading. Set the timer for one hour. Then, at the end of that hour, count how many pages you read and record the results. Repeat the process using the hourly page rate you accomplished in your most recent drill as the rate you want to improve on.

**ACTIVITIES
2.12–2.15**

Speed and Comprehension Drills

Improving your reading speed is of no value if your comprehension doesn't keep up. Comprehension—how well you understand and recognize important points in what you read—is essential to your success as a student.

In Activities 2.12 through 2.15, you will be asked to read several articles at a speed that will ensure 70 percent comprehension or better. As you read, you will learn about reading rates, the process of reading, poor reading habits, and developing a good vocabulary. The ten questions following each article will help you evaluate your comprehension skills.

If your instructor is not timing these exercises, you will need a watch, clock, or timer. Time yourself, and record your time. Your goal is to improve your time—even as the activities get longer. After you read, answer the questions, and check your paper for comprehension errors using the answer key in the appendix at the end of this unit. Score your work by adding a zero to the number correct. Then, on a separate sheet of paper, make a chart entitled "Comprehension Activities" like the one that follows, and record your time and score.

COMPREHENSION ACTIVITIES

	1	2	3	4	5	6	7	8	9	10
Time										
Score										

Speed and Comprehension Drill 1

ACTIVITY 2.12

Read "What Is Your Reading Rate?" and answer the questions that follow the article. Time yourself, or ask your instructor to time you. Record your time on your Comprehension Activities chart.

What Is Your Reading Rate?

If someone asks you "What is your reading rate?" you can be sure that person knows very little about reading. It is incorrect to assume a person has just *one* reading rate. Although research shows the average high school student reads an average of 250 words per minute, the really good reader knows reading rates need to be *flexible*.

Some students think that, if they read everything slowly, they will achieve maximum comprehension. However, they are wrong. In fact, sometimes reading so slowly has the opposite effect because it lulls those people into daydreaming. Their brains are not being challenged. Successful readers learn to read quickly when it is warranted and slowly when it is necessary.

So, what determines the correct reading speed? Three factors determine it. The first is the difficulty of the material. If the material you are reading is complex, you must slow your reading speed. If the material is easy and entertaining, you can speed up your reading. The second factor is purpose. *Why* are you reading the material? If you are reading it to prepare for a quiz the next day, you'd better slow your pace. If you are reading it for pleasure, then you can speed up. Finally, the third factor that determines reading speed is familiarity with the subject matter. If the material and the concepts are new to you, then slow down your reading to take them in. If you are already familiar with the concepts in the material, then speed up. Good readers, learn to vary their speed from 150 to 800 words per minute, choosing their appropriate speed after considering all three factors: difficulty, purpose, and familiarity.

Number from one to ten on a separate sheet of paper. Beside each number write *true* if the statement is true and *false* if the statement is false.

1. Everyone has *one* personal reading rate.
2. High school students read an average of 250 words per minute.
3. Reading slowly assures a student of maximum comprehension.
4. The difficulty of the material is a consideration when choosing a reading rate.
5. A very difficult selection should be read at 250 words per minute.
6. A light, entertaining selection should be read at 250 words per minute.
7. Almost everyone reads material for a quiz at a slower speed than material for relaxation.
8. An astronomy expert can probably read an article on astronomy at a faster rate than someone who knows nothing about the subject.
9. Before selecting your own reading rate, you should consider the average reading rate of others in your class.
10. One of the major points made in this unit is that reading rates must be constantly changing.

ACTIVITY 2.13

Speed and Comprehension Drill 2

Read the article entitled "How Do You Read?" and answer the questions that follow it. Time yourself, or ask your instructor to time you. Then record your time.

How Do You Read?

 Most students probably assume that when they read, their eyes follow in a straight motion across the lines of print, like this:

Eyes follow the print in a straight line.

That is not so. You need only to sit across from someone and carefully observe his or her reading process to discover:

The eyes move in an arc across the lines of print.

Each time the eyes reach the bottom of the arc, they pause, or stop to take in words. These pauses are called *fixations*. It is only at the fixation point that your eyes see words. When the eye is making the arc, the motion is rapid; in fact, it is so rapid the reader is unaware of it. Only your brain "sees" the rapid blur of the arc. It is fortunate that as you read you do not see the arc—it would cause a terrible headache! As your eyes go through the motions of reading, they are in the arc 6 percent of the time; 94 percent is spent at the points of fixation.

Slow readers move their eyes in the word-by-word arc illustrated above. It is easy to see why slow readers tire easily and become discouraged. Reading is a difficult process for them.

Fast readers, on the other hand, read more fluently.

Fast readers take in 2.5 to 3 words per fixation, making the task of reading a much simpler one. Our goal in this unit is to use the rapid discrimination exercises as beginning drills to expand the amount of letters, and then words, you can take in per fixation. You begin with as few as four *letters* per fixation. With practice, you can work up to 2.5 to 3 *words* per fixation. This skill will help you be a better reader and will save you time, as well.

Number from one to ten on a separate sheet of paper. Beside each number write *true* if the statement is true and *false* if the statement is false.

1. A fixation is a pause or stop of the eyes to take in words.
2. A reader's eyes do not move in a straight line when reading.
3. Fifty percent of a reader's time is spent in motion between words, and 50 percent is spent fixating.
4. An inefficient or slow reader takes in one word per fixation.
5. An efficient reader takes in four to five words per fixation.
6. The eyes of a slow reader make an arc every 2.5 to 3 words.
7. The eyes of an efficient reader make an arc covering one word at a time.
8. Readers are aware of the blur made when their eyes make the arc motion from one fixation to the next.
9. The blur made by the arc motion causes some people to get frequent headaches when reading.
10. There is no difference between the amount of effort a slow reader puts forth while reading and the amount of effort a fast reader puts forth.

Speed and Comprehension Drill 3

ACTIVITY 2.14

Read the following article and answer the questions. Time yourself, or ask your instructor to time you. Then record your time; are you improving?

Reading Habits That Slow You Down

As you work to build your speed in reading, be alert to four common reading habits that may slow you down.

The first, *vocalizing*, is mouthing or saying the words aloud as you read them. It is easy to spot someone who has this problem. And vocalizing *is* a problem, because the act of mouthing or speaking slows you down; it takes too much time to say the words with your lips. There are several ways to help yourself stop vocalizing. Try chewing gum or holding a pencil clenched between your teeth as you read. Or, put your hand over your mouth or keep it at your throat to feel for vibrations of vocalizing.

Unfortunately, the second problem reading habit is much harder to detect. It is called *subvocalizing*, and it is characterized by a reader's forming the words in his or her larynx. In order to avoid pronouncing internally the words you read, practice reading rapidly under timed conditions, or talk about the material to yourself.

The third problem reading habit is *pointing*. When you point with your finger or a pencil or a ruler, you add another mechanical step to the reading process. This can only slow you down. The solution is to make pointing impossible by folding your hands in your lap.

The last problem reading habit is *head movement*. Following the lines of print with your head does not increase reading speed. Like pointing, it adds another mechanical step to the reading process. To avoid it, hold your chin in your hand, or place your hand against the side of your head.

Once you are aware that these reading habits can slow you down, you can begin improving your reading speed on a daily basis. Be aware that an exception to the total elimination of these habits might be when you are reading difficult materials. Vocalization, subvocalization, and following along with a finger may help some people remember complex information.

Number from one to ten on a separate sheet of paper, Beside each number write *true* if the statement is true and *false* if the statement is false.

1. *Vocalizing* is mouthing the words when reading.
2. Vocalizing does not slow a reader's speed; it just distracts others.
3. Chewing gum while reading is a cure for vocalizing.
4. Subvocalizing is like vocalizing; the words are said aloud for everyone to hear.
5. Reading rapidly under timed conditions is a cure for subvocalizing.
6. Pointing with your finger helps you keep your place and improves your reading speed.
7. Pointing with a pencil or ruler is preferred to pointing with a finger.
8. Moving your head to follow the lines of print slows your reading speed.
9. A cure for head movement is to hold your hand against the side of your head as you read, so that you can feel any head movement.
10. There are only four reading problems people need to consider.

ACTIVITY 2.15

Speed and Comprehension Drill 4

Read the article entitled "Vocabulary Affects Speed and Comprehension" and answer the questions that follow. Time yourself, or ask your instructor to time you. Record your time, then compare it to your time on the first drill.

Vocabulary Affects Speed and Comprehension

The previous comprehension activity focused on four common reading problems that affect reading speed. A fifth problem is a poor vocabulary. If you stumble over words, or you have to stop and think about them, your reading speed is slowed. Developing a good vocabulary will help you improve both your reading speed and your comprehension.

One way to improve your vocabulary is to read a lot. The more you read, the more words you will encounter, and the more your vocabulary will grow.

You can also improve your vocabulary by paying attention to new words. Instead of skipping over it, stop and figure out what a new word means. Use context clues from the sentence, if possible.

If context clues don't help, look up the meaning of the word in your dictionary. Then make a special effort to learn it. Using the new word in your writing or conversations will help you remember it.

Keeping a vocabulary notebook will also help. Although writing down the new words and their meanings takes more time, the benefits to you will make your efforts well worthwhile.

If possible, get involved in an organized vocabulary program in class. Use a vocabulary workbook and complete at least one lesson per week. Your vocabulary will grow if you make a genuine effort to learn and use the words in each lesson.

Finally, become aware of root words, prefixes, and suffixes. In *Speedreading for Better Grades*, Ward Cramer states it is possible to double your vocabulary by learning no more than a couple dozen prefixes.

Of course, the key to developing your vocabulary is by *being aware* of new words, by *discovering* their meanings, by *committing* them to memory, and by *using* them in your conversations.

Number from one to ten on a separate sheet of paper. Beside each number write *true* if the statement is true and *false* if the statement is false.

1. Developing a good vocabulary will help your reading speed but not your comprehension.
2. The more you read, the more your vocabulary will grow.
3. Using clues within a sentence to determine the meaning of a word will help increase your vocabulary.
4. Context clues are the clues to a word's meaning given by the sentence or paragraph in which the word appears.
5. The process of looking up a word's definition in the dictionary is sufficient for learning that word.
6. Using a new word in your conversation with others does not help you learn the word.
7. Keeping a vocabulary notebook takes too much time, and the payoffs aren't worth it.
8. Completing lessons in a vocabulary workbook pays off in an increased vocabulary.
9. Learning a couple dozen prefixes will double your vocabulary.
10. Learning root words is a waste of time for vocabulary building.

Review

Unit 2

I. True-False (1–10)

Number your paper from one to ten. Read the following statements. Write *true* if the statement is true or *false* if the statement is false.

1. A knowledgeable and efficient reader reads all materials at the same rate.
2. Reading rate is not affected by having a good vocabulary or a poor one.
3. One way to build a good vocabulary is to read a lot.
4. You can build a good vocabulary by using the dictionary to look up meanings of words you don't know.
5. One way to build a good vocabulary is to use new words frequently in writing and conversations.
6. To build a vocabulary, you should skip over a word you do not know, unless it appears more than once in your reading.
7. To build a good vocabulary, keep a vocabulary notebook.
8. Learning common prefixes, suffixes, and roots of words can help you build your vocabulary.
9. Your eyes move in a straight line across the lines of print as you read.
10. Reading rates are much the same from one person to the next.

II. Multiple Choice (11–14)

Number your paper from eleven to fourteen. Place the letter of the correct answer beside the corresponding number on your paper.

11. Reading speed is determined by which of the following:
    A. your purpose.
    B. your background.
    C. the level of difficulty.
    D. A, B, and C

12. A *fixation* is a pause or stop of the eyes to take in words as you read. How many words does a slow reader take in at one fixation?
    A. one
    B. two
    C. three
    D. none of these

13. How many words does a fast reader take in at one fixation?

    A. one

    B. one to two

    C. two or more

    D. none of these

14. How many words does an efficient reader take in at one fixation?

    A. 1.0 to 1.5

    B. 2.0 to 2.5

    C. 2.5 to 3.0

    D. none of these

III. Matching (15–21)

Four common reading faults are listed in the left column, and cures for each are listed in the right column below. Number your paper from fifteen to twenty-one. Choose the cure(s) for each fault and write the answer(s) beside the correct number on your paper.

15.–16. Vocalization (pronouncing each word)—Two cures	A. Fold your hands and let your eyes do the work.
17.–18. Subvocalization (nothing visible; words are formed in the larynx)—Two cures	B. Place your hand against the side of your head.
19.–20. Head movement—Two cures	C. Chew gum as you read.
21. Pointing with finger, pencil, or pen—one cure	D. Talk about the problem to yourself.
	E. Hold a pencil clenched between your teeth.
	F. Read rapidly under timed conditions.
	G. Hold your chin firmly in your hand.
	H. None of the above.

IV. Short Essay (22–23)

22. Discuss the value of the rapid discrimination drills and whether they have helped you. If they have helped, explain how; if they haven't, explain why not.

23. Discuss what you learned in Unit 6 about reading speed (and comprehension). How can you apply this knowledge to your own reading skills?

Answers to Rapid Discrimination Drills 1–10

Activity	1	2	3	4	5	6	7	8	9	10
Question: 1	4	4	2	1	2	1	2	3	4	1
2	5	4	3	3	5	1	4	5	3	3
3	2	2	2	2	3	3	3	1	3	2
4	3	3	3	4	1	4	1	4	4	5
5	5	5	3	5	4	2	5	2	3	4
6	1	4	2	2	1	1	2	4	1	2
7	3	1	1	1	2	2	4	1	1	1
8	1	2	4	5	3	2	1	3	4	3
9	2	5	1	4	5	2	3	5	2	5
10	4	1	2	3	4	2	5	2	4	4
11	5	4	4	1	2	1	1	2	2	2
12	3	5	2	5	4	4	3	4	4	1
13	1	3	2	3	1	3	2	1	2	3
14	4	4	1	4	3	4	3	3	4	5
15	2	2	3	2	5	1	4	5	2	4
16	5	3	2	3	1	4	1	2	2	4
17	3	1	3	1	2	1	5	4	4	2
18	4	4	2	4	3	3	2	1	3	1
19	1	5	3	2	3	4	3	3	2	3
20	2	1	2	5	4	3	4	5	1	5

Answers to Comprehension Questions 1–4

Activity	6.12	6.13	6.14	6.15
Question: 1	false	true	true	false
2	true	true	false	true
3	false	false	true	true
4	true	true	false	true
5	false	false	true	false
6	false	false	false	false
7	true	false	false	false
8	true	false	true	true
9	false	false	true	true
10	true	false	false	false

Skimming and Scanning

You already have been introduced to the idea that you read different materials at different rates of speed. For example, you would not read *Mad* Magazine at the same speed that you would read a letter from a lawyer about an inheritance from a distant aunt. Different speeds should be used for different purposes when reading. If you are reading everything at the same rate, you are wasting your time!

Unit 3 focuses on the range of your reading rates. Do you read at speeds of 100 to 200 words per minute (wpm)? Do you think you can read at speeds of close to 1,000 wpm? You are about to discover the answers to these questions.

You will begin with a slow and careful rate and advance through the rapid and very rapid rates achieved in skimming and scanning. The range of your reading rates may surprise you.

Flexible Reading Rates

ACTIVITY 3.1

First you need to be aware that there *are* different reading rates. You may be surprised at just how flexible your current rates are. For instance, without realizing it, you probably use different rates to skim the newspaper and scan the phone book than you use to read this textbook.

On a separate sheet of paper, begin a section of notes entitled "Skimming and Scanning." Read the selection "Reading Rates Should Be Flexible," and answer the following questions. Remember, for better memory retention and re-call, be sure to write both the questions and the answers.

Skimming and Scanning

1. What three things determine your reading rate?
2. What is *scanning?* When should you use it?
3. What is *skimming?* When should you use it?
4. When should you use a rate that is rapid? Very rapid? Average? Slow and careful?
5. What two factors influence reading rates?

Reading Rates Should Be Flexible

If someone asks you "What is your reading speed?" you can assume that he or she doesn't know much about reading. Reading everything fast or slow is the sign of a poor reader. If you are a good reader, you have several different reading rates.

A good reader shifts from one rate to another according to the following considerations:

1. What is the *purpose* of your reading? Are you studying or reading for pleasure? Are you getting a general overview, or are you looking for specific facts?
2. How *difficult* is the material to comprehend? Is it hard or easy for you to read the selection?
3. How *familiar* is the subject matter to you? Is this all new material or do you have some background in the subject?

Good readers use many different rates. If you have never thought about this, you will be surprised to learn that good readers switch from one rate to another as they need to. No conscious thought process is used; they just switch automatically.

Let's consider the rates involved in skimming and scanning. In *skimming,* you get an overview or hit only the major points of the material. You read the first few paragraphs, then glance over the remaining material, noting the chapter headings and words in bold type. Skimming is useful for getting acquainted with a new text, for choosing suitable reference material for a report, or for selecting a book from the library. Your skimming rates might range from 800 to 1,000 words per minute (wpm).

In *scanning,* you glance at material until you find a particular piece of information. When you look for a telephone number, or you find a particular date in a history book chapter full of dates, you scan. Your scanning rate might be 1,000 to 1,500 wpm or more.

Clearly, skimming and scanning are valuable skills for you to acquire. They have many practical uses.

You range of reading rates will include the following:

1. Very rapid—perhaps 400 wpm. Used for light, entertaining reading, such as fast-moving fiction.

2. Rapid—perhaps 350 wpm. Used for fairly easy material from which you need only the more important facts.

3. Average—perhaps 250 wpm. Used for most of the material read in daily life and for some school work.

4. Slow and careful—perhaps 200 down to 50 wpm. Used for thorough reading, to remember details, difficult concepts, and vocabulary.

You may need to shift from one reading rate to another within the same article or chapter. Good readers can do it without even thinking about it. For example, you might read the beginning of an article at an average rate, as you are being introduced to its contents. But as you proceed, a step-by-step technique is outlined, and you would switch to a slow and careful rate to increase your memory retention. At the end of the article, the author might restate the major points covered. Again you would shift gears, returning to an average of fairly rapid reading rate, depending on your familiarity with the material.

Remember that your reading rates are extremely personal. Although you may have a variety of rates that you have learned to use easily, the speeds you can attain are not the same as those of another person. Temperament and intelligence also influence reading rates. With practice, you will learn what reading rates work best for you.

Skimming and Scanning

ACTIVITY 3.2

In Activity 3.1 you were introduced to the concepts of skimming and scanning. You may have been surprised to find that you already use these techniques in your everyday life without even thinking about it. But you do use these same tools in your academic pursuits? If you do not, you are wasting valuable study time. Skimming and scanning are reading techniques you should use when you study.

For example, do you reread the entire chapter the night before a test? Instead of wasting your study time doing that, use the skimming technique to review the chapter. Skimming has another practical academic use: If you were not able to read the chapter in time for class discussion, try previewing or overviewing as an emergency measure.

In Activity 3.2, you will learn about three specific techniques: previewing, overviewing, and reviewing. They will increase your ability to read only the parts that you need to know for a particular situation.

Begin by reading the selection entitled "Skimming and Scanning." On a separate sheet of paper, add to your notes on this topic. Then define the following new terms: *preview; review; overview*. Be sure to include examples of their uses.

Skimming and Scanning

You have already done a number of activities that focused on the skill of reading materials at different rates. Learning how to vary the rate at which you read is invaluable. It will not only save you time, it will also increase your comprehension.

You have already been introduced to two types of very rapid reading.

- **Skimming:** passing quickly over an entire selection to get a general idea or "gist" of its contents. For example, you skim a chapter in your history book to review your knowledge of the Civil War.

- **Scanning:** glancing at a selection for a specific piece of information and stopping when you find it. For example, you scan the *S* column in the telephone book looking for Joe Santiago's number.

The major difference, then, between skimming and scanning is that, when you finish skimming, you have covered the entire selection briefly; in scanning, you glance only until you find what you are looking for, and then you stop.

Skimming and scanning both involve reading selectively. In other words, you read only those parts that will serve your purpose. Skimming, however, involves three basic forms of selective reading—previewing, overviewing, and reviewing.

- **Previewing:** The prefix *pre* means before; to preview is to view the material *before* you actually begin reading it. Previewing is usually followed by a more thorough reading. You can use previewing to select a book, survey a chapter, or search for appropriate research material.

- **Overviewing:** Overviewing is getting a "big picture" view of the material. Overviewing usually is *not* followed by another reading. You use overviewing to get an overall sense of the content of an article or book.

- **Reviewing:** The prefix *re* means *again*. When you review, you view the material again. Reviewing follows a previous reading. You can use reviewing to go back over material to refresh your memory, especially before a test or important discussion.

Skimming and scanning are both done rapidly. Remember, though, that they differ in purpose and length.

ACTIVITIES
3.3–3.7

Your Personal Reading Rates

Now that you understand about flexible rates and varying purposes for reading, you will have an opportunity to see just how greatly your reading rates can vary. Intellectually, you know that you don't read everything at the same speed. As you follow the instructions for the reading rate samples, you will see just how different the rates really are.

You will begin by examining and recording your *slow and careful* rate—the rate you use when you study or when you want to remember specific details. Next, you will have an opportunity to use and record your *average* rate. This rate is used when you want to recall main ideas. A faster rate may be used when you are reading for pleasure. Recording your skimming speed will tell you how fast your *rapid* or "once over lightly" rate is. Your scanning rate will be *very rapid*, since you race along looking for a specific item when you scan. As you compare the different speeds, you will realize how variable your reading rates are.

Reading Rate Chart

You will need a chart for recording your reading rates. Divide a sheet of paper into two columns. Label the columns with the headings shown in the illustration. Be sure to leave plenty of room to record times and answer questions. You will use this chart for Activities 3.4 through 3.8.

First you will record the time you begin reading; then the time you stop reading. Next, answer the comprehension questions.

After you have answered the questions, subtract the time you began from the time you stopped to find your total reading time.

Example: Time stopped 2:30
Time began   <u>2:22</u>
Total time   :08

Next, turn to page 52 to find the number of words per minute you read.

READING RATE CHART

Time	Minutes	Seconds
Activity 3.4 **Slow and Careful**		
Time stopped	_____	_____
Time began	_____	_____
Total time read	_____	_____
Words per minute	_____	
Score	_____	
Activity 3.5 **Average**		
Time stopped	_____	_____
Time began	_____	_____
Total time read	_____	_____
Words per minute	_____	
Score	_____	
Activity 3.6 **Rapid**		
Time stopped	_____	_____
Time began	_____	_____
Total time read	_____	_____
Words per minute	_____	
Gist of article:		
Activity 3.7 **Very Rapid**		
Time stopped	_____	_____
Time began	_____	_____
Total time read	_____	_____
Words per minute	_____	
What does it mean to "learn your boss's management style"?		

Slow and Careful Reading Rate

Before you begin reading the article "Creating Successful Study Habits," note the time and write it on your paper. (For greater accuracy, if your instructor is not timing you, use a watch or clock with a second hand.)

Read this article as a *slow* and *careful* rate for maximum comprehension. The material you will be reading is similar to that in a textbook, and you will be given a test over specific details from the article.

When you finish reading, again note and record the time. In order to compute the total amount of time you spent in reading the selection, subtract the time you began reading from the time you stopped. Next, consult the conversion chart on page 52 in order to record your reading rate in words per minute.

To measure your comprehension, without looking back at the article, answer on a separate sheet of paper the ten true-false questions in the Comprehension Test section. Check your answers; then compare your score by multiplying your number correct by ten.

Creating Successful Study Habits

Webster's Dictionary states that a habit is something done often and easily. The word *often* should be emphasized whenever speaking about developing study habits. The habits that will help you be most successful in your studies are the ones that you repeat daily both at school and at home.

You should practice the following study habits daily.

1. Use an assignment sheet in every class.
2. Write down all assignments in full detail.
3. Read the assignment sheets after the end of your class, but *before* leaving school.
4. Bring home all the books, worksheets, folders, and notebooks needed to complete the homework.

If you want to study and complete assignments successfully at home, you must develop these study habits *at school*. After all, the most common excuses for not finishing or doing homework are that the book was left at school or that the assignment was forgotten. You won't forget if you develop the study habits that help you remember these important items.

The study habits that will help you at home include the following.

1. Begin your homework at the same time every night.
2. Do your work in the same place each night.
3. Ask your parents or guardians to help you maintain a positive work environment.

Once again, you must repeat this routine every night in order to make these successful study habits. Common homework hassles such as difficulty getting started or failing to allow enough time to finish the work are avoided by starting the work at the same time each night. Your starting time should allow at least one and one-half hours for completing the assigned work.

Where you do your work should also become a habit. Always doing the work at the same location breeds success in several ways. First, it helps you get started on your work at the same time each evening. Supplies you use often, such as paper, pen, pencil, ruler, and eraser, can all be stored at or near your study area. Thus, you avoid a time-consuming and distracting hunt for these items each night.

Your work area should be well lit and should include a large flat surface. It should also be as free of noisy distractions as possible. The most common distractions are televisions, radios, stereos, ringing telephones, and younger brothers and sisters. Every distraction makes it harder to complete the work and do it well.

In addition, the encouragement and support of a parent or guardian constitutes an important aspect of creating good study habits. Ask a parent to get in the routine of not only asking if you have homework, but also asking to see your day's assignment sheet. You parent might help by quizzing you, or by assisting with any problems you encounter with an assignment. He or she might also review your completed work.

You'll finish your homework more quickly and efficiently if you adopt and practice the study habits discussed here. With self-discipline and dedication, you, too, can be a good student.

Below are ten questions. Read each one carefully. Then, on a separate sheet of paper, write the correct answer beside the appropriate number. Do not look back at the article. When you finish, check your answers and multiply your number correct by ten. Record your comprehension score on your paper.

1. You should use an assignment sheet in:
   A. every class.
   B. some classes.
   C. important classes.

2. You should use the assignment sheet:
   A. often.
   B. daily.
   C. occasionally.

3. You should read the assignment sheet:
   A. at the end of each class period.
   B. after your last class ends, but before you leave school.
   C. before you start your homework at night.

4. Beginning homework at the same time each night:
   A. helps you get started more easily.
   B. provides you with enough time to finish everything.
   C. both of the above

5. Your starting time should allow you:
   A. a half hour of study time each night.
   B. one hour of study time each night.
   C. one and one-half hours of study time each night.

6. Doing your work in the same place each night:

    A. helps you get started at the same time each night.

    B. avoids delay because all your supplies are there.

    C. both of the above

7. According to the author, distractions should be avoided because:

    A. they slow you down.

    B. they make it harder for you to complete the work and do it well.

    C. both of the above

8. A parent might help by:

    A. asking if you have assignments.

    B. asking to see your assignment sheet.

    C. both of the above

9. A parent can also help by:

    A. quizzing you on your work.

    B. reviewing your completed work.

    C. both of the above

10. You will benefit from the study habits discussed in this article if you practice them:

    A. the evening before a test.

    B. at least three evenings each week.

    C. every evening.

ACTIVITY 3.5

Average Reading Rate

Let's go on to consider average reading to determine your rate in words per minute. You will be using a light, entertaining selection that you can read at a faster rate than the previous article. However, do not read so fast that you lose comprehension.

Note the time and write it on your paper. Then begin reading. When you finish reading, again note the time and record it. Subtract the time you began from the time you stopped to determine the total time read. Turn to the Conversion Chart on page 52 to compute your words read per minute, and record this figure. Then take the comprehension test for this story.

Mary Had a Little Lamb

It's a little-known fact of nature that sharks are not the only animals which have feeding frenzies. The slightest hint of a milk bottle will send orphan (bum) lambs wild. They will stampede, trampling any hapless bystanders in the dust. Anyone brave enough to try feeding two bottles to more than two lambs will have fingers chewed, ears nibbled, and noses bitten. The mere presence of a known food supplier will turn a field of angelic bum lambs into a frenzied mob. Yet, there are some compensations to owning bums if you can solve the feeding problem. Pincushion is an example.

Pincushion and his sister Giraffe entered the world on a chilly, blustery March day. Preemies, they were too weak to stand, too small to have reached their mother if they could have stood. Only my timely arrival saved them being put out of their misery by my husband, Chris, who thought they would never survive. I took them home to see if I could save them, while my husband gave the grieving ewe a new lamb who needed a mother.

Giraffe we named immediately. She had a long delicate face and looked for all the world like a miniature giraffe. Pincushion's name came later.

Once home I began the process of warming the half-frozen lambs. They were immersed in comfortably hot water and fed a small amount of brandy to warm their insides. After they were briskly rubbed dry, I gently forced colostrum milk down their throats with a needleless syringe. They were too weak to suck from a bottle.

Within two hours they could raise their heads and were placed in their new home—our bathtub with a rug in the bottom. Within four hours they had developed pneumonia, and the fight for their lives began. They were each given three shots—two antibiotics and a stimulant. Feeding continued every three to four hours. Shots were administered daily.

By the third day we seemed to have conquered the pneumonia. It looked as though we were going to save them. Then scours (diarrhea) hit them. The needles came out again. More medicine was administered, and Pincushion earned his name. None of our other bums had ever been given this many shots in this few days.

When the crisis passed, the lambs gained enough strength to stand and take faltering steps. We cheered their progress around the house. They began to suck a bottle of milk and rapidly became family pets.

These lambs weighed perhaps a pound a piece when they were born. Their legs resembled matchsticks. Their heads were as fine as a fawn's, and their emaciated bodies were painful to see. By the time they were two weeks old, their bodies had begun to fill out. My husband wanted his tub back. It was time to move the lambs to our lamb nursery.

In an old house we owned, we had set up a straw-lined pen for newborn bums. Pincushion and Giraffe were installed in this pen. Tragically, Giraffe's delicate constitution could not withstand the transition. Soon we were fighting a losing battle with pneumonia.

While Giraffe struggled to keep a spark of life, Pincushion grabbed hold of life. His small size allowed him to slip through the sides of his pen. Once outside he mingled with lambs six to ten times his size. Mealtimes were trample time for Pincushion. He was always on the bottom of the pile but always fighting his way toward the top.

Time and time again we placed him back in the nursery, plugging more holes each time. Time and time again we picked him up from the bottom of the heap when we returned to feed the bums. Finally, we left him with his friends.

When Pincushion was about a month old we put a self-feeder in with the lambs. we were tired of having our fingers gnawed at feeding time. As soon as we saw that the bums had the hang of things, we left to complete our other chores. When we returned, Pincushion lay on the floor moaning and writhing in agony.

His belly was distended to three times its normal size. He was a victim of his own gluttony.

With tears in my eyes I moved Pincushion back to his old bathtub to die in peace, I closed the shower curtains and left him there while I went to town for an appointment. I knew nothing I could do to ease his agony, and I could not stand to see the end.

When I returned and threw back the shower curtains, Pincushion was gone. "Well," I thought, "he died, and Chris has taken the body away." Some need to say "good-bye" drove me to search the trash can—no Pincushion. "Chris probably took him somewhere so that I didn't have to see him"—my thoughts were interrupted by a faint bleating. I hurried to a small outdoor pen, and there Pincushion stood demanding to be fed.

The rest of the story I heard from Chris. He had stopped at the house to pick up the body a few hours after I left. He was sure that the lamb would have died by then. Instead he was greeted at the door by a vigorous Pincushion, wanting food. He replaced Pincushion in the tub and closed the curtains, but before he could leave the bathroom, Pincushion was out of the tub and at his heels. That is when Pincushion was transferred to the outdoor pen.

When Pincushion could be trusted to digest all he could eat at the self-feeder, we transferred him back to the bum pen. Although the tiniest of all the lambs, once he grabbed a nipple at the feeder no lamb could ever dislodge him. He sucked until the last drop of milk was gone, oblivious of the other lambs who pushed, shoved, crawled over and under him. He thrived, grew, and finally became the leader of the bums.

Pincushion outgrew many of the bums and lived a long, pleasant summer with us. We never lacked for companionship when Pincushion was near. He followed at our heels, nudged us to be petted, and nuzzled us with affection.

We sold Pincushion in the fall. There is no room on a modern farm for a nonproducing animal. We turned our heads and could not look at this gentle friend and companion. We were ashamed that scarce dollars dictated the fate of Pincushion.

In his short time with us, he was a model of bravery, indomitable courage, perseverance and friendship. Tucked away with all my memories of good and fine things is the memory of Pincushion.

To measure your comprehension, without looking back at the article, answer the following ten questions. On a separate sheet of paper, write the letter of the correct answer beside the appropriate number. When you finish, check your answers and multiply your number correct by ten. Record your comprehension score on your paper.

1. A bum lamb is a lamb that is:

    A. deformed.   B. sick.   C. an orphan.

2. The sight of _____ will send angelic lambs into a frenzied mob.

    A. their mother   B. a milk bottle   C. hay

3. Pincushion and Giraffe were sick because they were:

    A. cold.   B. preemies.   C. ignored.

4. In order to save the lambs, the author:

   A. immersed them in comfortably hot water and rubbed them dry.

   B. fed them a small amount of brandy and colostrum milk.

   C. both A and B

5. The first new home for the lambs was:

   A. a bathtub.   B. a playpen.   C. an old house.

6. The lambs had to battle:

   A. pneumonia.   B. scours.   C. both A and B

7. The lamb that showed the greatest will to survive was:

   A. Pincushion.   B. Giraffe.   C. neither A nor B

8. Pincushion battled for survival a fourth time because of:

   A. the cold.   B. greed for food.   C. the other lambs.

9. Pincushion survived because of:

   A. loving care.   B. a strong spirit.   C. both A and B

10. The author:

   A. cared very much for the lambs.

   B. was happy to sell the lambs and take a profit.

   C. wondered why she spent so much time with the lambs.

Rapid Reading Rate

ACTIVITY 3.6

The next reading rate we will focus on is skimming. There is a technique to skimming efficiently. Try it on the article entitled "Guidelines for Succeeding with Your Boss."

A. Read the title.

B. Read the introduction (first four paragraphs).

C. Read the ten rules (headings only).

D. Read the conclusion (last two paragraphs).

   Begin by noting the time and writing it on your chart. Then skim "Guidelines for Succeeding with Your Boss," using the method outlined above.

   When you finish, record the time you stopped; then subtract the time you began from the time you stopped to determine the total time read. Turn to the Conversion Chart on page 52 to compute your words read per minute.

   Next, to check your comprehension, write a brief paragraph explaining the gist of the article.

Guidelines for Succeeding with Your Boss

All the books and articles on how to make good at work usually ignore one very basic premise in "how to get ahead." This practical bit of wisdom never seems to come up in polite conversation, although every employee from the office assistant to the vice president is well aware of it.

Figure Out What the Boss Wants   There is no mystery to this; it is really only common sense. Find out how your boss likes to be dealt with and learn how to do it. You will both benefit.

Here are ten guidelines for getting along with your boss that surveyors of management methods have gleaned from their work with bosses of all types.

1. *Be professional.* Bosses set the tone for the degree of formality or informality that they are most comfortable with in the workplace. Also, as a general rule, to avoid embarrassment for one or both of you, personal problems are usually best left at home.

2. *Respect them and their authority.* Remember that the buck stops with them. They are ultimately responsible for every success or failure. Don't challenge their right to tell you what to do or to judge what you have done. They are paid to do just that. It is their job.

3. *They are in touch with the whole picture.* You deal with only one aspect of the company's business. Their scope of responsibility is much greater than yours. They may, in turn, report to several bosses instead of one, as you do.

4. *Is your timing appropriate?* At what time of the day is your boss most receptive to new ideas? When is he or she most likely to be irritable? Be aware of your boss's schedule. Think about what might be happening in the company that will demand his or her undivided attention. Then plan your time with your boss accordingly.

5. *Learn their management style.* Some bosses delegate a lot of authority. Others do not. Some bosses expect to be consulted about everything. Others expect you to do your job on your own, once you have instructions. Some bosses are very formal in their manner, while others are more relaxed and friendly. Learn all you can about your boss's style.

6. *Find out how they prefer to be contacted.* Can you drop by anytime, or do you need an appointment? Can you do your business over the phone, or does your boss prefer that you sit down across the desk from him or her?

7. *They are only human.* Many people expect their bosses to be perfect and then complain when they are not. Remember, bosses make mistakes and say things without thinking just as you do. They also may have other things on their minds when you approach them. Recognize that they, too, are human, and you will avoid much anxiety and misunderstanding when some days do not go as smoothly as you would like.

8. *Keep them aware of what goes on.* This is the highest priority for many bosses surveyed. They want to know who, what, why, when, and where. They need to know these five Ws in order to plan ahead, make decisions, and report to their own bosses. When you are reporting to them about something, be sure to learn whether they like to know all the details or want

only general information. Also remember that bosses like to learn good news as well as the bad. It may be a pleasant change.

9. *Don't try too hard to please the boss.* To constantly try to please makes you less than a favorite among your co-workers, and you probably spend more time with them than with your boss, anyway. There's an old saying that "cream always rises to the top." Your path will be smoother if, on the way up, you get along with others.

10. *Bosses are individuals.* Keep this in mind when trying to understand them. They are not a company—they are real and unique people. Management techniques are helpful only if they relate to your particular boss.

You will benefit by learning about your bosses' management styles. Of course, the best way to succeed with your boss is to do your job well, but the extra effort it takes to learn more about his or her style of operating pays dividends for both of you.

Remember, if you look good, your boss looks good. Your ability to help your boss do his or her job better will lead you to even more success in the future.

ACTIVITY 3.7

Very Rapid Reading Rate

To conclude this survey of your reading rates, focus now on scanning, the fastest reading rate of all. Note the time you begin and write it on your chart; then turn back to page 50 and scan the article "Guidelines for Succeeding with Your Boss" to answer this question: What does it mean to "learn your boss's management style"?

As you finish, record the time you stopped; subtract your starting time from your stopping time and convert the result to words per minute using the chart on page 52. Answer the question briefly.

Now take a look back at the range of your personal reading rates. You may read at speeds of 100 to 200 words per minute or at speeds approaching or exceeding 1,000 words per minute. Whatever your rates, no doubt you'll agree: Your reading rate is flexible.

Conversion Chart for Reading Rates

COMPUTING READING RATES IN WORDS PER MINUTE

Slow and Careful	Average
"Creating Successful Study Habits"	"Mary Had a Little Lamb"
550 words total	1,120 words total

Slow and Careful

2 minutes = 276 words per minute
2:10 = 254 words per minute
2:20 = 236 words per minute
2:30 = 219 words per minute
2:40 = 206 words per minute
2:50 = 194 words per minute
3:00 = 183 words per minute
3:10 = 174 words per minute
3:20 = 165 words per minute
3:30 = 157 words per minute
3:40 = 150 words per minute
3:50 = 144 words per minute
4:00 = 138 words per minute
4:10 = 132 words per minute
4:20 = 127 words per minute
4:30 = 122 words per minute
4:40 = 118 words per minute
4:50 = 114 words per minute
5:00 = 110 words per minute

Average

3 minutes = 373 words per minute

3:10 = 358 words per minute	5:10 = 218 words per minute
3:20 = 343 words per minute	5:20 = 212 words per minute
3:30 = 328 words per minute	5:30 = 206 words per minute
3:40 = 313 words per minute	5:40 = 200 words per minute
3:50 = 298 words per minute	5:50 = 194 words per minute
4:00 = 280 words per minute	6:00 = 186 words per minute
4:10 = 271 words per minute	6:10 = 182 words per minute
4:20 = 262 words per minute	6:20 = 178 words per minute
4:30 = 253 words per minute	6:30 = 174 words per minute
4:40 = 244 words per minute	6:40 = 170 words per minute
4:50 = 235 words per minute	6:50 = 166 words per minute
5:00 = 224 words per minute	7:00 = 160 words per minute

Rapid Skimming

"Guidelines for Succeeding with Your Boss"

692 words total

:30 = 1,384 words per minute
:40 = 1,308 words per minute
:50 = 830 words per minute
1:00 = 692 words per minute
1:10 = 593 words per minute
1:20 = 519 words per minute
1:30 = 461 words per minute
1:40 = 415 words per minute
1:50 = 377 words per minute

Very Rapid Scanning

"Guidelines for Succeeding with Your Boss"

:10 = 2,400 words per minute
:20 = 1,200 words per minute
:30 = 800 words per minute
:40 = 600 words per minute
:50 = 480 words per minute
1:00 = 400 words per minute
1:10 = 343 words per minute
1:20 = 300 words per minute
1:30 = 266 words per minute

Skimming a Book

Any skills that save you time and make you a better reader are skills worth learning. Skimming and scanning will do just that. Try the following exercise using skimming to improve your rapid reading techniques.

Periodically, you will need to select a book for a project, report, or research paper, and you will have to look at several books before choosing the best one for the assignment. Knowing how to skim a book quickly will be a valuable skill. To give you practice in skimming for this purpose, select a book that pertains to a current research assignment. Or, choose a book from those provided for you by your instructor. Then use the following techniques to skim it.

1. Look at the title, author, and publication date. Has the book been reprinted? If so, how many times? Is the publication date recent enough to be appropriate for your research topic?
2. Read the publisher's comments on the cover or dust jacket.
3. Look at the preface or other introductory material.
4. Look at the table of contents (if there is one).
5. Look at the first chapter, using a skimming (previewing) technique.
6. Leaf through the rest of the book, looking at major headings, charts, pictures, graphs, and so on.

Now, on a separate sheet of paper, write a brief paragraph summarizing the contents of the book, and conclude with a statement of whether the book will be of value to you.

More Skimming and Scanning

The next four activities will give you practice in scanning. The activities are similar to those you might do in everyday situations at school or at work. Without scanning, these would become very time-consuming tasks. Imagine how long it would take to use the dictionary, telephone book, or encyclopedia if you had to start at the beginning and look at every entry until you came to the information you were seeking. Clearly, scanning is an essential reading technique.

Use a separate sheet of paper and a watch or clock with a second hand to time yourself if your instructor is not timing you. Be sure to note and record the time you begin and the time you finish each exercise. When you finish, subtract the time you started from the time you finished to compute the total time it took you to do the exercise.

Next, check your answers for accuracy and write a brief sentence explaining why this was an exercise in scanning. Can you see improvement as you compare your reading rates and the accuracy you achieved?

ACTIVITY 3.10

Listing Dates

Number a separate sheet of paper from one to fifteen, note and record the time, and begin. Arrange the following list of dates in order, starting with the least recent and ending with the most recent.

10/5/85	4/25/95	8–08–90
June 1, 1976	August 12, 1980	1/12/93
6–21–86	Nov. 4, 1990	2/14/94
January 25, 1989	12–25–94	March 17, 1987
May 1, 1992	7–02–82	September 5, 1991

Did you use skimming or scanning to do this exercise?

ACTIVITY 3.11

Commuter Train Schedule

For Activity 3.11, pay close attention to the column headings in the excerpt from a commuter train schedule in Figure 3.1. To read the timetables first note that the direction of the train (Harvard, Illinois, to Chicago, Illinois) and that the effective days of the week are indicated in the shaded areas of the schedule. Next, note that the train numbers are listed at the top of the timetables in this excerpt. Note where the various stations are listed. Follow across to the right to determine the departure time of each train. Note that you move down the schedule to determine the arrival time for each train at each station.

FIGURE 3.1   Commuter train schedule

Harvard to Chicago – Monday through Friday

CONNECTING SERVICES	PARKING	ZONES	STATIONS		602 AM	604 AM	606 AM	608 AM	610 AM	612 AM	614 AM	616 AM	618 AM	620 AM	622 AM	624 AM	626 AM
Pace	b	M	HARVARD	LV:	—	—	—	—	5:48	—	—	—	—	6:22	—	—	—
Pace	b	K	McHENRY	LV:	—	—	—	5:53	—	—	—	—	—	—	6:54	—	—
Pace	b*	K	Woodstock		—	—	—	6:02	—	—	—	—	—	6:38	↓	—	—
Pace	e*	I	Crystal Lake		4:50	5:20	5:40		6:14	—	6:18	6:35	—	6:50	↓	7:00	—
	c*	H	Cary		4:56	5:26	5:46		6:22	—	6:27		—	6:58	7:12	↓	—
	b*	H	Fox River Grove		4:59	5:29	5:49	↓	6:25	—	6:30		—	7:01	7:15	↓	—
Pace	e*	G	Barrington		5:07	5:37	5:57	6:18	6:34	6:27	6:38	↓	—	7:11	7:24	7:15	7:27
Pace	e*	F	Palatine		5:14	5:44	6:04	6:27	—	6:36	x6:47	6:56		x7:20		7:24	—
Pace	e*	E	Arlington Park		5:19	5:49	6:09	6:32	x6:43	6:41	x6:52	—	x7:11			7:29	x7:40
Pace	e*	E	Arlington Heights		5:23	5:53	6:13	6:37		6:46	x6:56	7:04	x7:16			7:33	x7:45
Pace	e*	D	Mount Prospect		5:28	5:58	6:18	6:42		6:51	x7:01		x7:22	↓		7:38	x7:50
Pace	c*	D	Cumberland		5:31	6:01	6:22	6:46	↓	—	x7:05	↓		x7:31	↓	7:42	x7:53
Pace	d*	D	Des Plaines		5:35	6:05	6:26		x6:54	6:56	x7:10	7:13			x7:41	7:45	x7:57
Pace	b	C	Dee Road		5:38	6:08	6:30			6:59	—	7:17			x7:45		x8:02
Pace, CTA Bus	d*	C	Park Ridge		5:41	6:11	6:33			7:02	x7:16	7:21			x7:50	↓	x8:06
CTA Bus	c	C	Edison Park		5:44	6:14	6:36			7:05		7:23				7:54	
CTA Bus	a	C	Norwood Park		5:47	6:17	6:39			7:08		7:26				7:58	
CTA Bus	a	B	Gladstone Park		5:50	6:20	6:42			7:11		—				8:01	
CTA Rail & Bus, Pace	b	B	Jefferson Park		5:53	6:23	6:45			7:14		7:32				8:04	
CTA Rail & Bus	b	B	Irving Park		5:57	6:27	6:49	↓	↓	7:19	↓	7:36	↓	↓	↓	8:08	↓
Metra CTA Bus	a	A	Clybourn		6:03	6:33	6:54	7:05	x7:11	7:26	x7:31	7:41	x7:46	x7:51	x8:05	8:14	x8:21
Metra CTA, Rail & Bus Amtrak, Wendella		A	CHICAGO Passenger Terminal AR:		6:12	6:42	7:03	7:14	7:19	7:35	7:40	7:50	7:55	8:00	8:15	8:24	8:30

PARKING: Number of spaces available at "a" is 50-99; "b",100-249; "c",250-499; "d",500-749; "e",750 or more.
Wendella Commuter Boat Service operates from late April through early October. For more information call (312) 337-1446.
X: Train stops on center track.   * Bicycle racks available.

FIGURE 3.1 Commuter train schedule (continued)

Harvard to Chicago – Monday through Friday cont'd

STATIONS		628	630	632	634	636	638	640	642	644	646	648	650	652	654	656	658	660	662
		AM	AM	AM	AM	AM	AM	AM	AM	PM	PM	PM	PM	PM	PM	PM	PM	PM	PM
HARVARD	LV:	—	7:08	—	—	7:35	—	9:35	—	—	1:35	—	—	4:35	—	5:35	—	8:35	—
McHENRY	LV:	—	—	7:36	—	—	—	—	—	—	—	—	—	—	—	—	—	—	—
Woodstock		—	7:23		—	7:48	—	9:48	—	—	1:48	—	—	4:48	—	5:48	—	8:48	—
Crystal Lake		—	7:36		—	8:00	9:00	10:00	11:00	12:00	2:00	3:00	4:10	5:00	—	6:00	8:00	9:00	11:59
Cary		—	7:43	↓	—	8:06	9:06	10:06	11:06	12:06	2:06	3:06	4:16	5:06	—	6:06	8:06	9:06	12:05
Fox River Grove		—	7:46	↓	—	8:09	9:09	10:09	11:09	12:09	2:09	3:09	4:19	5:09	—	6:09	8:09	9:09	—
Barrington		7:42	7:54	8:04	7:47	8:16	9:16	10:16	11:16	12:16	2:16	3:19	4:26	5:16	6:05	6:16	8:16	9:16	12:12
Palatine		x7:51			7:56	8:23	9:23	10:23	11:23	12:23	2:23	3:23	4:33	5:23	—	6:23	8:23	9:23	12:19
Arlington Park		x7:56			8:01	8:28	9:28	10:28	11:28	12:28	2:28	3:28	4:38	5:28	6:16	6:28	8:28	9:28	12:24
Arlington Heights		x8:01		↓	8:05	8:32	9:32	10:32	11:32	12:32	2:32	3:32	4:42	5:32		6:32	8:32	9:32	12:28
Mount Prospect				x8:18	—	8:37	9:37	10:37	11:37	12:37	2:37	3:37	4:47	5:37		6:37	8:37	9:37	12:33
Cumberland			↓		8:11	8:40	9:40	10:40	11:40	12:40	2:40	3:40	4:50	5:40	↓	6:40	8:40	9:40	—
Des Plaines				x8:12	8:14	8:44	9:44	10:44	11:44	12:44	2:44	3:44	4:54	5:44	6:24	6:44	8:44	9:44	12:38
Dee Road					8:17	8:47	9:47	10:47	11:47	12:47	2:47	3:47	4:57	5:47	—	6:47	8:47	9:47	
Park Ridge				↓	8:21	8:50	9:50	10:50	11:50	12:50	2:50	3:50	5:00	5:50	6:29	6:50	8:50	9:50	
Edison Park				x8:26	—	8:53	9:53	10:53	11:53	12:53	2:53	3:53	5:03	5:53		6:53	8:53	9:53	
Norwood Park					8:25	8:56	9:56	10:56	11:56	12:56	2:56	3:56	5:06	5:56		6:56	8:56	9:56	
Gladstone Park					8:28	—	—	—	—	—	—	—	—	—	↓	—	—	—	↓
Jefferson Park		↓	↓	↓	8:31	9:00	10:00	11:00	12:00	1:00	3:00	4:00	5:10	6:00	6:35	7:00	9:00	10:00	12:49
Irving Park		↓	↓	↓	8:35	9:04	10:04	11:04	12:04	1:04	3:04	4:04	5:14	6:04	6:40	7:04	9:04	10:04	
Clybourn		x8:26	x8:31	x8:42	8:44	9:11	10:11	11:11	12:11	1:11	3:11	4:11	5:21	6:11	6:47	7:11	9:11	10:11	↓
CHICAGO Passenger Terminal	AR:	8:35	8:40	8:51	8:53	9:20	10:20	11:20	12:20	1:20	3:20	4:20	5:30	6:20	6:57	7:20	9:20	10:20	1:08

Wendella Commuter Boat Service operates from late April through early October. For more information call (312) 337-1446.
X: Train stops on center track.

From the Metra (Union Pacific/Northwest Line) timetable, effective as of 1996.

For this activity, your speed in not important as your accuracy. You will use this type of information (transportation timetables) in everyday life as a commuter and as you plan to travel for yourself or for others.

Write your responses to the following questions on a separate sheet of paper. Use the train schedule provided in Figure 3.1 to answer the questions.

1. If you were going to Chicago, Illinois, from McHenry, Illinois, what is the earliest time you could leave in the morning?

2. How many stops are scheduled between McHenry and Chicago leaving at that time?

3. Which stations have between 250–499 parking spaces available?

4. How many stations have bicycle racks available?

5. If you are meeting a friend in the Chicago passenger terminal at noon, what time must you leave the Des Plaines station? What is the number of the train you need to take?

6. How many connecting service providers are listed? Which one provides limited service?

7. How long does it take to travel between Fox River Grove and Chicago if you take train number 638? Number 630?

8. At what time do the trains begin running each day during the week? When do they stop?

9. How many stops are scheduled at Gladstone Park? What is the number of the train that would allow you to arrive in Chicago before 8:30 A.M.?

10. What are the numbers of the last two trains you could board in Barrington in order to arrive in Chicago before 8:30 A.M.?

Skimming, to review, means reading through an entire selection quickly to get a general idea of its content. Many students find skimming to be one of the most useful techniques they have learned; it will be valuable to you as well. Besides saving you time, skimming also improves your comprehension. In fact, skimming followed by actual reading can double comprehension.

How much information can you get just by skimming something? You will get an opportunity to compare test scores on information you skim with test scores on information you read completely. Both tests will use the same material.

Remember, when you master skimming, you will be able to preview, review, or overview material quickly and easily. This technique will be invaluable for both school and work situations.

In order to skim efficiently, use the following method.

1. Read the title of the selection.
2. Read the first paragraph.
3. Read the first sentence of each of the other paragraphs.
4. Read the final paragraph.

Use a separate sheet of paper. Label it as shown below.

Skimming		Actual Reading	
Time stopped	_____	Time stopped	_____
Time began	_____	Time began	_____
Total time	_____	Total time	_____
Words per minute	_____	Words per minute	_____
Score	_____	Score	_____

ACTIVITY 3.12

Skimming

If your instructor is not timing you, use a watch or a clock with a second hand to note the times you start and finish each exercise. Record these times on your paper. When you ar ready, or when your instructor gives the signal, begin reading "Cycling's Risks" using the skimming technique described previously in Steps 1 to 4. When you finish with the exercise, subtract the time you started from the time you stopped to determine the total time used. Then turn to the Conversion Chart (page 60) to figure the number of words per minute. Next, number a separate sheet of paper from one to ten and answer the Comprehension Test questions.

ACTIVITY 3.13

Actual Reading

Now read the entire article entitled "Cycling's Risks." Record the times you begin and finish. Subtract your beginning time from your finishing time to find total time read; again, turn to the Conversion Chart on page 60 to convert the results to words per minute. Take the Comprehension Test again, writing your answers on a separate sheet of paper. Also, now that you have read all of the article, make any changes you want to in your answers to the first Comprehension Test you took after using skimming.

For each test (after skimming and then after actual reading), multiply your number correct by ten to get your percentage scores. Record these scores in the appropriate blanks. Now compare them. How many answers did you change? (If you scored 70 percent or better on the skimming test, you are using skimming very effectively.) Notice how much information you got simply by skimming. Did you notice skimming helped you improve your comprehension when you did the actual reading of the article? You will find skimming beneficial with many kinds of reading materials.

Cycling's Risks

My noncycling friends think bike racers are crazy. They can't believe how long road races are. If they get on a bike and try to sustain 20 mph they become exhausted. As a result they are flatly incredulous when I tell them that races go at 25 to 28 mph for several hours. Sprinters' hills loom like mountains in their minds and the Mt. Evans Hill Climb is simply unimaginable. When I assert that the training which brings such performances within reach is enjoyable rather than agonizing, they nod knowingly to one another.

But these doubters reserve their most vehement attacks on my sanity for what they perceive as the unacceptable dangers of cycling. Recently a friend picked up an old copy of a racing publication and read about Alan Kingsbery's near-fatal collision with a truck crossing a time trial course. When he finished he looked at me searchingly. "How can you justify your sport," he said, "when you have a wife and son?"

I did not consider the question idle, presumptuous, or even rhetorical. I have asked it of myself at times, especially after crashes or close calls. Certainly there are safer activities for a person in his thirties who has heavy responsibilities in life. But because I enjoy cycling so much, I find it easy to justify—what dangers there are seem eminently worth the risk. Yet part of me realizes that my justifications are not the real reason I ride in spite of the hazards. Consider how easily I can find excuses to ignore the danger:

> Given the state of automobile accident statistics, I am probably at least as safe when racing, commuting, and training as I would be in a car.
>
> Wearing a hardshell cycling helmet cuts down on the risk of serious injury and fatality. And I wear one at all times, not just when racing.
>
> We have to take some calculated risks in life. Man is by nature a risk-taker, a challenger of limits, or he would not have evolved. In fact, the whole evolutionary history of life is a history of the risks that nature takes when minute individual differences are introduced into the species. Many of these fail, but some are successful and lead to improved adaptation to the challenges of life. In the same way, an individual human life without risk would

result in a stagnant personality. Thoreau was right: When it comes time for me to die, I do not want to look back on my life and find that I have not lived.

Racing helps me to stay fit. The alternative, a sedentary lifestyle, is more deadly than any danger faced while cycling. Of course, I could get fit by swimming, but I have no talent for it— I would probably drown (that really is an unjustifiable risk). Serious running, for me, is unhealthy. My knees can rarely handle runs over twenty miles and my hips get sore at random, apparently just to be contrary. Although it may be argued that I could maintain my fitness by recreational cycling and avoid the sport's dangers, I see commuting, training, and racing as part of the whole experience. Each reinforces and gives meaning to the others until the composite attitude toward transportation, health, enjoyment, and competition merges into a lifestyle.

I am safer in cycling than in other sports I could choose. I played football enthusiastically and with abandon for ten years, but the major injury and death statistics from that sport continue to appall me. After college I got involved in mountaineering. I still have recurring visions of a basketball-size boulder bounding at me down a couloir on Crestone Needle. It missed; my knees shook for an hour. When I downhill ski it is either me or the mountain and I've never won yet. I could become a motorcycle racer, a cliff diver, a Pipeline surfer or an Indy driver. In comparison to many sports, not to mention wars to everyday household accidents, cycling is outrageously safe.

Even though all these arguments roll glibly off my tongue, responsibility to family remains a disturbing and pertinent point. However, I would rather take a small and calculated risk to be a fit, alive, interesting, and exuberant cyclist than come ponderously home each evening to the TV and snack tray. The risks of such a lifestyle may be less obvious than those of racing, but they are more insidious, more deadly and, to my mind, far less acceptable. In the end I can easily justify my cycling: We cannot choose the time and manner of our deaths, but we can have a say in the style and quality of our lives.

But to list reasons why I can accept the dangers of cycling is merely to eliminate the negative. Trying to justify cycling by checking off the debits ignores the positive reasons for racing and training that overwhelm the drawbacks.

My reasons for racing do not arise out of a simplistic view of competition. I rarely taste the thrill of victory; as for the agony of defeat, I try to keep my performances in proper perspective. Racing is certainly not my whole life, nor do I wish it to be. When I am honest with myself I realize that I race for three reasons, all compelling, but none noble or unselfish.

I race because I hate pain. I know that such an admission, besides sounding like a paradox, is inconsistent with the cliché of the macho cyclist picking gravel out of grisly abrasions while gritting his teeth on a spare crankset bolt, but it is true. The longer I have been involved in sports, the more fascinated I have been by my reaction to pain. I have become addicted to the process of facing that pain and trying to beat my fear and loathing. The result is now a post-race euphoria that is only slowly replaced by accelerating anxiety about the next contest. Aristotle may not have been a bike racer, but he knew about fear and pain. He called it catharsis: a combination of pity, terror, and relief. He was talking about the audience's reaction to tragedy, but it is applicable to us moderns as we experience self-inflicted "sports pain"—pity for ourselves at the specter of approaching pain, terror that it will hurt so much we'll quit or slow down and get dropped, and finally relief that the demon has been met face to face and conquered, or at least confronted honestly. In the weekly cycle of quiescence, anxiety, competition, and catharsis, my fear and hatred of pain is purged.

I also race because I like to ride with other people—sometimes. Since I live far from the area where most of Colorado's races and riders are located, I usually train alone. I prefer it that way because I can ride when it fits my schedule. But part of the thrill of cycling is how bikes handle around other bikes: the vacuum, suction, lightening sensation of a big pack, the psychedelic patterns of alloys and jerseys, the sense of shared enterprise and momentary alliances, the way the pack develops a mind and will of its own, independent of, and yet connected to, each rider's perceptions and personality. Nowhere is this better experienced than in a race where individuals merge into one sinuous group while still maintaining their separate wills and motivations and personalities. When I train alone, I clear my head of all the trivia of the day. But when I am in a pack of riders, I feel a part of the race sharing the hopes, dreams, and honest fears of everyone else.

Finally, I simply like to ride a bicycle and racing gives me an excuse to do it often. I don't need to justify my riding to other people, but when daily tasks press hard on the time I set aside for me, it helps to be able to justify it to myself.

On a separate sheet of paper, write *true* if the statement is true or *false* if the statement is false.

1. Noncyclists think bike racers are to be admired for their bravery.
2. Noncyclists think cycling is dangerous.
3. Fred Matheny, the author of this article, feels he is as safe when cycle racing as when riding in a car.
4. Matheny feels wearing a helmet offers very little protection from serious injury.
5. The author believes in taking risks to some degree.
6. He feels he is safer in cycling than in playing football or in downhill skiing, but not as safe as when swimming.
7. Matheny prefers to ride with others all the time.
8. Matheny uses racing as an excuse to ride his bike simply because he loves to ride it.
9. The author periodically considers giving up bicycle racing because of the dangers involved and because he hates pain.
10. Matheny thinks about bike racing's dangers versus his responsibility to his family.

CONVERSION CHART: SKIMMING AND ACTUAL READING

"Cycling's Risks"

1,110 words total

30 sec = 2,220 words per minute	3:50 min = 287 words per minute
40 sec = 1,666 words per minute	4:00 min = 275 words per minute
50 sec = 1,325 words per minute	4:10 min = 264 words per minute
1:00 min = 1,110 words per minute	4:20 min = 254 words per minute
1:10 min = 943 words per minute	4:30 min = 244 words per minute
1:20 min = 827 words per minute	4:40 min = 236 words per minute
1:30 min = 733 words per minute	4:50 min = 227 words per minute
1:40 min = 662 words per minute	5:00 min = 220 words per minute
1:50 min = 601 words per minute	5:10 min = 212 words per minute
2:00 min = 550 words per minute	5:20 min = 206 words per minute
2:10 min = 507 words per minute	5:30 min = 200 words per minute
2:20 min = 472 words per minute	5:40 min = 194 words per minute
2:30 min = 440 words per minute	5:50 min = 188 words per minute
2:40 min = 413 words per minute	6:00 min = 183 words per minute
2:50 min = 388 words per minute	6:10 min = 179 words per minute
3:00 min = 366 words per minute	6:20 min = 175 words per minute
3:10 min = 347 words per minute	6:30 min = 171 words per minute
3:20 min = 330 words per minute	6:40 min = 167 words per minute
3:30 min = 314 words per minute	6:50 min = 163 words per minute
3:40 min = 300 words per minute	7:00 min = 159 words per minute

On a separate sheet of paper, number from one to twenty-five. Follow the directions for each section of the review and write your answers beside the corresponding numbers on your answer sheet.

I. Vocabulary Terms (1–9)

Use the following terms to identify the type of reading described below:

skimming	review	overview
scanning	very rapid reading	slow and careful reading
preview	rapid reading	average reading

1. This follows a previous reading and is used when you go back over material to study for a test or to prepare a report.

2. Moving quickly over an entire selection to get the gist of it is _____.

3. This is most often followed by a second reading; it is used in selecting a book, surveying a chapter before reading it, and so on.

4. This rate is used when covering difficult concepts and vocabulary, when reading technical material, and when it is necessary to retain every detail.

5. This rate is used for light, easy, and entertaining reading.

6. When you glance over material very quickly until you find a desired piece of information, and then you stop reading, you are using _____.

7. A reading to get a general impression of the material is a(n) _____; it is not followed by another reading.

8. This rate is used for magazine articles or some chapters in social studies and is about 250 words per minute.

9. This rate is for fairly easy material and when you want only the more important facts.

II. Completion (10–18)

Write the correct answer in the corresponding space on your answer sheet.

10–12. Your reading rate is determined by three factors. They are __10__ , __11__ , and __12__ .

13–14. Two other factors that influence your own ability to read rapidly are __13__ and __14__ .

15–18. The four steps in skimming an essay, a chapter, or a book are __15__ , __16__ , __17__ , and __18__ .

III. Application (19–25)

The following are descriptions of material you might encounter and the purposes you might have for reading it. Read the description and the purpose. Then select the appropriate reading rate from the list provided. Write the rate you have chosen beside the corresponding number on your answer sheet.

scanning   very rapid   average
skimming   rapid   slow and careful

Type of Material	Your Purpose	Rate
19. The chapter in a social studies textbook on Reconstruction after the Civil War	You need to understand completely. A test on details is coming up.	?
20. A light, fast-moving Louis L'Amour story, *Buck, the Cowboy Renegade*	You are reading for pleasure.	?
21. An encyclopedia article on the life of Herbert Hoover	You want to know what college President Hoover attended.	?
22. Your English teacher has made the following assignment: List the characteristics of a good writer.	You need to research several articles to locate the parts that list the characteristics. You will read them more carefully later.	?
23. An interesting adventure story in a magazine	You are reading in the dentist's waiting room to pass the time.	?
24. You bought a new car. You are considering what type of insurance to buy.	You want to understand fully the extent of the coverage you need.	?
25. Local news in your paper	You want to know what's going on in your town.	?

Reading for Enjoyment

How long has it been since you read something for relaxation or fun? For many people, reading for pleasure is a rare treat—a chance to catch up on sports news, to learn how to do a weekend project, or to get caught up in a mystery or science-fiction fantasy.

As you read and complete the activities in this unit, you will have opportunities to read your local newspaper, browse through a magazine, or get lost in a good book. The most important goal is to rekindle your enthusiasm for reading for pleasure.

Begin your reading for pleasure by sitting down with a copy of your local newspaper. Some of you will read metropolitan papers; others will read papers from small towns. As you read, notice the unique style of your local newspaper. Compare its format to that of one of your classmate's newspapers. Notice how the writing style varies from reporter to reporter. You'll find that newspapers contain a wealth of information beyond advice columns, the comics, and the sports section. Avid reader or not, you will learn from and enjoy reading your local newspaper.

Newspaper Survey

ACTIVITY 4.1

This activity will help you evaluate your reading habits regarding the daily newspaper. Using a separate sheet of paper, write your responses to the Newspaper

Survey that follows. Your instructor may ask you to share your responses so you can compare your reading habits with those of your classmates.

Newspaper Survey

1. What newspaper(s) do you read?
2. How frequently do you read a newspaper?
3. What time of the day do you read the newspaper?
4. Indicate which newspaper sections you read and how often you read them by writing the name of the section and *always*, *usually*, *sometimes*, or *never* after each section you list.

front page	features
sports	classified ads
editorials	general ads
business	weather
comics	obituaries

5. If you didn't have the opportunity, would you miss reading the newspaper? If so, why?

ACTIVITY 4.2

Newspaper Jargon

There are some common terms used frequently by people discussing the newspaper. Knowing these terms will help you understand and actively participate in this part of the unit.

On a separate sheet of paper, write the terms that follow and their definitions. Then locate an example of each term in the newspaper of your choice. The terms listed below will appear in the Unit Review, so be sure your notes on them are complete and accurate.

1. Banner Headline: a headline that stretches across the newspaper page from one side to the other.
2. Headline: large type above an article indicating the content of the article.
3. Byline: a line at the beginning of an article listing the author's name.
4. Dateline: a line indicating where the event described in the article took place.
5. News Agency: an organization that sends news stories by wire. Two of the most well-known news agencies are the Associated Press and Reuters.
6. AP: the abbreviation for *The Associated Press*.
7. Lead: an article's first paragraph, in which the questions *who*, *what*, *when*, *where*, and *why* (the five Ws) are answered.
8. Caption: the words beside or below a photograph or illustration that give information about the picture.
9. Jump: words informing a reader that an article continues on another page.

Sections of the Newspaper

Take a minute and try to name all the sections you would find in an average newspaper. If you are the type of reader who skips from the front page to the sports section to the comics, you might have trouble with your list. This activity will help you discover *all* of the sections in your newspaper.

First, from the following list read the name of your newspaper section and its description. Add this information to your notes. Then, using a newspaper and its index, find that particular section. In your notes, write down the location in your newspaper of each of the sections given.

Sections of the Newspaper

Front Page: the page a reader sees first. Its format, appeal, and contents often influence a reader's decision about whether to buy the paper. Thus, the front page helps sell the paper; it also carries the most important stories of the day.

Editorial Section: Presents opinions through editorials by staff writers; editorial cartoons; letters to the editor (written by readers); and syndicated columns.

Feature Section: Entertains and appeals to readers' interests through comics; information on and reviews of movies, plays, concerts, and celebrities; home-making hints; fashion news; and so on.

Sports Section: Covers a wide variety of sporting events and includes analyses of player and team performances; coaching strategies; scheduled games; statistics; predicted winners; and so on.

Business Section: Consists of articles that discuss and analyze economic activity; personnel; business strategies; and companies of note. It also includes stock quotations and interest rates.

Advertising Section: Pays those who produce the newspaper; allows businesses to communicate with consumers; informs readers of products and services available in the marketplace.

Weather Section: Includes local or regional forecasts; describes road conditions; lists national temperatures and extended forecasts.

Obituary Section: Contains notices of the deaths of prominent persons, usually members of the community, but sometimes national or international figures. It usually includes brief accounts of the persons' lives and may include lists of surviving family members and funeral information.

Analyzing the Newspaper

Too often people limit their newspaper reading to only a couple of sections. For example, when you read a newspaper, you may consistently read only the front page, the comics, and the list of automobiles for sale. But you may be missing valuable information by doing this, as Activity 4.4 will show you.

Using a newspaper and its index, locate the sections of the newspaper discussed in Activity 4.3 in order to discover what type of information is contained in each section. Then, on a separate sheet of paper, answer the following questions.

Front Page

1. What is the title of the most important story on the newspaper's front page?
2. Does the front page have one or more pictures? Does it include an index?
3. How many articles appear on the front page?

Editorial Section

1. Does the editorial section contain letters to the editor? Editorial cartoons? Syndicated columns?
2. List the topic of one of the editorials written by a staff writer.

Feature Section

1. Does the feature section include a TV schedule? A movie schedule? A review of a movie? Comics? Hints for homemakers? Fashion news? Advice columns such as "Dear Abby" or "Ann Landers"?

Sports Section

1. Does the sports section include a sports cartoon? Team standings? Reports of past games? A story about an important person in sports? A column by a sports writer?
2. On what pages do you find sports information?

Business Section

1. Does the business section list stock quotations from the New York Stock Exchange? The American Stock Exchange? The NASDAQ?
2. Does the section contain articles about important people in business? Specific companies? List the names of the companies featured.
3. Does the section contain syndicated columns? A report on grain prices? Money market rates?

Advertising

1. On what pages do you find the classified ads?

Weather

1. On what pages is the weather discussed?
2. Does the weather section contain forecasts? Road conditions? National temperatures?

Obituaries

1. On what pages do you find the obituaries?
2. Do any of the obituaries include pictures?
3. How many obituaries are listed in today's section?

Exploring the Front Page

Remember that a newspaper's front page is very important, especially on the newsstand. It must sell the paper. What do you know about the front page of today's newspaper? Use it to help you answer the questions that follow. Write your responses on a separate sheet of paper.

1. What is the headline of today's top news story?
2. How many columns does the front page of your newspaper have?
3. Does your newspaper print the weather news on the front page?
4. Does your newspaper print an index on the front page?
5. How many front page news stories contain a jump?
6. How many front page stories have been circulated by news agencies? How many are from the A.P.? How many are from Reuters?
7. How many photographs appear on the front page?
8. How many headlines on the front page of today's newspaper take up more than one column?
9. Does the front page contain a banner headline?
10. How many front page stories contain bylines?
11. How much does your newspaper cost?

Exploring the Editorial Pages

You probably take time to read your newspaper's front page, but its editorial pages may be new to you. The editorial pages present opinions of the newspaper's editorial staff, opinions of syndicated columnists from across the country, and opinions of the general public. By reading the editorial pages, you encounter new viewpoints. Whether you agree or disagree with what is being expressed, the editorials will make you think more about your position on the issue.

Using a separate sheet of paper and today's newspaper, turn to the editorial section and answer the following questions.

1. Find the editorials written by the newspaper's editorial staff. List headlines from two of them.
2. Choose one of the two editorials, explain the staff writer's viewpoint, and then discuss your viewpoint.
3. Find the *letters to the editor* and list the topics of two of the letters.

4. Choose one of the letters to the editor, explain how the author felt about the topic, and then discuss your feelings.

5. Study one of the editorial cartoons and then explain its theme.

6. Find two syndicated columns. List the headline, author, news agency, and topic of each.

ACTIVITY 4.7

Scavenger Hunt in the Classified Ads

Have you ever scanned the classified ads hoping to find a used car bargain or a part-time job? Perhaps you have written a classified ad of your own. Individuals who want to buy, sell, rent, or trade something can place classified ads in the newspaper. These ads produce revenue for the newspaper and serve as a clearing-house for community commerce as well.

Using the classified section from a newspaper, answer on a separate sheet of paper the following questions. You will need to locate and use the classified ad index to find the appropriate section for each question. Have fun while you are on your scavenger hunt...some of the ads are very interesting!

1. What is the most unusual item that has been lost?
2. How many motorcycles are for sale?
3. Which used car would you buy if you had your choice?
4. Which "personal" ad do you find the most interesting?
5. What job would you apply for if you were job hunting?
6. How many yard sales are listed?
7. Which two pets would you adopt if you had room in your home?
8. Which business opportunity interests you most?
9. Which number(s) would you call for a day care center that welcomes "drop-ins"?
10. What should you do if you find an error in an ad you placed?

ACTIVITY 4.8

Writing a Classified Ad

Many people use classified ads to advertise items they would like to sell; many of these same people are surprised at the response their ads receive. A well-written classified ad can help you empty your garage and pad your wallet. To write an effective ad, there are a few basic principles you need to know, however. Above all, keep in mind that people skim ads quickly, so remember:

1. The first word of the ad should catch a reader's attention.

This:	Not This:
FIREWOOD, del. and stacked. Mixed pinion, oak, and pine. $72/cord. 555-6858	OLD So. Cntry. kindling, fat pine—great gifts. For free brochure write Brewton Inc. P.O. Box 555, Brewton, Pa.

2. Use as few words in the ad as possible, because the cost of placing a classified ad is determined by the length of the ad. However, you must be certain that the ad includes all necessary information.

This:

1 BDRM, carpet, drapes, appl.,
adults, no pets; $275 + utilities.
555-0425

Not This:

CHEERFUL!
Near bus, utilities, $185,
555-1064.

3. In a classified ad, abbreviations are fine—if a reader can understand them. A brief ad that makes no sense to its readers cannot be effective.

This:

PENTAX C330 with 45mm,
60mm, 180mm lenses $595.
Yashica with 85–250mm Zuika
lens, $250. 555-1786

Not This:

PENTAX 6x7, 35, 75, 105,
135 mm XT, WL, EL, $1,175.
Mike 555-7373.

4. Finally, be sure your ad is placed in the appropriate category in the classified ads. If you have a car to sell, place your ad in the "Automobiles for Sale" category, not "Miscellaneous."

Using the Classified Index shown on this page and keeping in mind the principles for writing good ads, compose two classified ads for things you would like to buy, sell, or rent.

```
                 CLASSIFIED INDEX
Real Estate . . . . . .1   Wanted   . . . . . . . .8
Rentals . . . . . . . .2   Help Wanted . . . . . .9
Rentals Wanted  . . . .3   Jobs Wanted  . . . . .10
Service Offered . . . .4   Lost & Found . . . . .11
Household Goods . . . .5   Personals   . . . . . .12
Miscellaneous . . . . .6   Motorcycles   . . . . .13
Pets  . . . . . . . . .7   Automobiles   . . . . .14
```

Sports Line

ACTIVITY 4.9

Thousands of avid sports fans read the sports section each day, and if you are among them you will surely enjoy this activity. Use the sports section of your newspaper to answer the questions that follow. Write your responses on a separate sheet of paper.

1. What is the headline of today's top sports story?
2. Does one sport receive more coverage today than the others? If so, what sport is it? Why do you think that sport is given more attention?
3. Do upcoming games get more coverage than those already played?
4. What are the titles of the standings and statistics columns?

5. List all the sports in today's sports section that are given any type of coverage.

6. Did you read any articles that you thought showed the bias of the sports writer? Which team does he or she seem to prefer? How could you tell?

7. Are there any feature stories in today's sports section? If so, what topic do they discuss?

8. Is there any coverage of women's sports? If so, which ones?

9. Is there any high school sports coverage?

10. Are there any predictions of winners? If so, for which sport? List the name of the column or article in which the prediction was made.

FIGURE 4.1
NBA Standings

NBA STANDINGS

WESTERN CONFERENCE
Midwest Division

	W	L	Pct.	GB	L10	Strk	H	A	Cnf
Houston	24	8	.750	—	4-6	L 2	12-6	12-2	17-5
Utah	23	8	.742	½	5-5	W 1	16-2	7-6	14-6
Minnesota	14	18	.438	10	6-4	W 2	10-4	4-14	10-12
Dallas	10	19	.345	12½	2-8	L 2	6-7	4-12	7-9
San Antonio	9	21	.300	14	6-4	L 1	5-9	4-12	7-16
DENVER	8	23	.259	15½	3-7	L 4	4-11	4-12	6-12
Vancouver	6	26	.188	18	3-7	L 4	5-12	1-14	4-13

Pacific Division

	W	L	Pct.	GB	L10	Strk	H	A	Cnf
L.A. Lakers	24	9	.727	—	8-2	W 5	14-2	10-7	15-5
Seattle	23	11	.676	1½	7-3	W 2	11-4	12-7	16-6
Portland	18	15	.545	6	5-5	W 4	9-6	9-9	15-10
L.A. Clippers	13	19	.406	10½	6-4	W 3	7-9	6-10	11-11
Golden State	12	18	.400	10½	5-5	W 1	8-8	4-10	7-12
Sacramento	13	20	.394	11	5-5	L 3	9-8	4-12	9-13
Phoenix	10	22	.313	13½	3-7	L 3	7-8	3-14	7-14

EASTERN CONFERENCE
Atlantic Division

	W	L	Pct.	GB	L10	Strk	H	A	Cnf
Miami	24	8	.750	—	7-3	L 1	8-5	16-3	14-6
New York	23	9	.719	1	7-3	W 1	14-4	9-5	14-6
Washington	16	15	.516	7½	6-4	W 1	8-8	8-7	9-11
Orlando	11	17	.393	11	2-8	L 1	7-7	4-10	9-11
New Jersey	8	21	.276	14½	3-7	L 3	5-9	3-12	4-17
Philadelphia	8	22	.267	15	1-9	L 4	4-10	4-12	5-13
Boston	7	23	.233	16	2-8	W 1	6-10	1-13	3-16

Central Division

	W	L	Pct.	GB	L10	Strk	H	A	Cnf
Chicago	28	4	.875	—	9-1	W 3	15-1	13-3	18-3
Detroit	24	7	.774	3½	7-3	W 4	15-3	9-4	20-5
Cleveland	21	10	.677	6½	8-2	W 3	15-4	6-6	11-9
Atlanta	18	11	.621	8½	7-3	W 2	11-1	7-10	12-10
Charlotte	17	14	.548	10½	5-5	L 1	9-5	8-9	11-11
Milwaukee	15	16	.484	12½	3-7	L 5	9-9	6-7	10-10
Indiana	14	16	.467	13	5-5	L 1	6-6	8-10	7-10
Toronto	10	21	.323	17½	3-7	L 3	9-8	1-13	7-16

Sports Scoreboard

In the sports section of your newspaper, you will find many tables like the one shown in Figure 10.1. As you can see, all the teams in the National Basketball Association (NBA) are listed with their standings. There are two divisions in each conference. The conferences are divided by geographic location. This table shows wins, losses, percent of wins, and the number of games back a team is from first place. Refer to the table to answer the following questions. Write your answers on a separate sheet of paper.

1. What are the names of the two divisions in the Eastern Conference?
2. List the names of the divisions in the Western Conference.
3. Which team is in first place in each of the four divisions?
4. What statistic do the San Antonio, New Jersey, and Toronto teams have in common?
5. Which four teams were "in the cellar" when these standings were current?
6. Which team in first place looks most impressive to you? Why?
7. Which of the teams in last place looks best at this point in the season? Why?

Forecasting the Weather

Are you going to a football game, baseball game, track meet, or tennis match? You can use the temperatures and forecasts given in the weather section of your newspaper to help you decide what clothing to wear to be comfortable. If you are going to travel across the state, or go on a vacation to another area of the country, the weather section's predictions and present temperature lists will help you choose what to pack. The weather is a constant source of news, and the following activity will help you discover what types of weather information your newspaper provides.

Often, on the front page of a newspaper you can find a brief summary of the local weather forecast. The summary shown in Figure 4.2 is typical, giving information about the weather forecast for the day and evening.

For more detailed information, you would consult the official weather maps distributed by the National Weather Service. These maps appear daily in most newspapers. Such things as areas of low and high atmospheric pressure, position and movements of large air masses, and storm activity are illustrated as in Figure 4.3. Usually, this same information is summarized in a paragraph that you can find somewhere near the map.

Weather

DENVER AREA: Variably cloudy, not so cold and a few snow showers today. Partly cloudy, snow showers ending and cool tonight. Highs, 33-38; lows, 15-20. Details on Page 12-C.

FIGURE 4.2
Weather Forecast
Summary

FIGURE 4.3   Detailed Weather Forecast

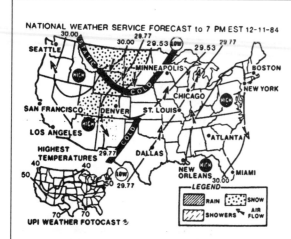

NATIONAL WEATHER SERVICE FORECAST to 7 PM EST 12-11-84

UPI WEATHER FOTOCAST

LEGEND: RAIN, SNOW, SHOWERS, AIR FLOW

Cold, snow showers predicted for area

The unseasonably mild temperatures that have graced the Denver area will be replaced Tuesday by cold air and snow showers, weather forecasters said.

Ron Kelly, the Rocky Mountain News forecaster, said a storm front would move through the metropolitan area Tuesday, bringing overcast skies and rain that would change to snow in the late afternoon.

The forecast called for 1 to 2 inches of snow in the area overnight, and from 4 to 8 inches in the mountains, Kelly said. Highs for Tuesday were expected to be in the high 40s, dropping to 18 to 20 degrees Tuesday night.

Kelly said the cold weather would remain at least through Wednesday.

ROAD CONDITIONS

U.S. 6 west — Loveland Pass: icy in spots, snowpacked. I-70 west — Eisenhower Tunnel (both approaches): wet. Vail Pass: icy in spots. Glenwood Springs: icy in spots. U.S. 24 Colorado 91 — Fremont Pass: icy in spots. Tennessee Pass: wet, icy in spots. U.S. 40 west — Rabbit Ears Pass: wet, icy in spots, snowpacked in spots. Steamboat Springs: wet, icy in spots. U.S. 50 & 550 west of 285 — Monarch Pass: icy in spots. Red Mountain Pass: wet, icy in spots, snowpacked in spots. U.S. 160 west — La Veta Pass: icy in spots. Wolf Creek Pass: icy in spots, snowpacked in spots.

For updated road conditions, call the Colorado Department of Highways at 639-1111 for Denver and roads west, and 639-1234 for I-25 and roads east.

For mountain and avalanche conditions, call 236-9435 in Denver and Boulder; 482-0457 in Fort Collins, 688-5485 in Frisco, 827-5687 in Vail, and 920-1664 in Aspen.

FIGURE 4.4   Local and State Data

LOCAL AND STATE DATA

Monday's temperatures
Airport observations

High . . . . 63 degrees
Low . . . . 23 degrees
Mean temp. was . . . . . . 3 degrees

For the record
Normal high for Monday 47
Normal low for Monday 20
Record high for Monday 74
set in 1939.

Monday's air quality at 5:15 p.m.: 213.
Tuesday's air quality forecast: extremely poor.

Record low for Monday . . . . . -13
set in 1932.
Humidity high on Monday 74
Humidity low on Monday 16

Sun and moon
Tuesday's sunrise 7:12 a.m., sunset 4:36 p.m.
Tuesday's moon rises 7:33 p.m., sets 10:15 a.m.

Precipitation to 6 p.m.
Precipitation for Monday . . . 0.00 inches
Precipitation this month . . . . . trace
Normal for month . . . . 0.55 inches
Precipitation since Jan. 1 . . . 16.03
Normal precip. since Jan. 1   14.96

Last qtr.   New   1st qtr.   Full
Dec. 15   Dec. 22   Dec. 30   Jan. 6

DENVER'S MONDAY HOURLY READINGS

Hour	Temp.	Humidity
midnight	35	59
1 a.m.	34	59
2 a.m.	31	66
3 a.m.	31	65
4 a.m.	31	63
5 a.m.	30	63
6 a.m.	26	74
7 a.m.	26	74
8 a.m.	31	58
9 a.m.	34	64
10 a.m.	43	51
11 a.m.	54	24
noon	58	20
1 p.m.	61	17
2 p.m.	62	16
3 p.m.	62	20
4 p.m.	57	25
5 p.m.	50	37
6 p.m.	44	43

nr — no report

COLORADO TEMPERATURES

City	Hi	Lo	Prc
Alamosa	48	5	
Boulder	nr	nr	
Colo. Springs	58	25	
Craig	nr	nr	
Denver	63	23	
Dinosaur	nr	nr	
Durango	54	nr	
Fort Collins	51	20	
Glenwood Spgs	38	21	
Grand Junction	38	32	
Greeley	55	21	
Gunnison	nr	nr	
La Junta	59	25	
Lamar	nr	nr	
Leadville	48	5	
Limon	58	23	
Pueblo	57	20	
Salida	nr	nr	
Sterling	nr	nr	
Trinidad	65	31	
Vail	nr	nr	

FIGURE 4.5   Temperature Listings

NATIONAL TEMPERATURES

		Mon Dec 10			Tue Dec 11			Wed Dec 12	
City	Lo	Hi	Prc	Wea	Lo	Hi	Wea	Lo	Hi
Albany	22	38	.00	Ptcldy	30	45	Ptcldy	27	48
Albuquerque	27	52	.00	Ptcldy	31	54	Ptcldy	34	53
Amarillo	29	66	.00	Ptcldy	29	72	Ptcldy	37	50
Atlanta	47	63	.00	Sunny	45	67	Sunny	43	68
Atlantic City	47	53	.00	Ptcldy	40	50	Ptcldy	37	54
Austin	51	75	.00	Ptcldy	51	77	Cloudy	53	76
Baltimore	39	50	.00	Sunny	37	53	Sunny	34	58
Billings	38	56	.00	Snow	20	35	Ptcldy	15	44
Birmingham	55	66	.00	Sunny	40	67	Sunny	45	70
Bismarck	19	40	.00	Windy	24	26	Ptcldy	01	28
Boise	28	42	.08	Ptcldy	27	40	Snoshw	31	40
Boston	31	49	.21	Ptcldy	40	48	Ptcldy	37	50
Brownsville	56	82	.00	Ptcldy	58	84	Ptcldy	60	84
Buffalo	36	46	.07	Ptcldy	35	48	Cloudy	39	49
Burlington Vt	31	40	.00	Ptcldy	29	41	Ptcldy	28	46
Casper	35	40	.00	Snow	27	39	Ptcldy	07	34
Charleston Sc	48	62	.00	Ptcldy	44	67	Sunny	45	71
Charleston Wv	37	52	.41	Sunny	39	55	Ptcldy	34	60
Charlotte Nc	30	48	.06	Sunny	36	60	Sunny	35	66
Cheyenne	23	55	.00	Cloudy	25	45	Cloudy	11	35
Chicago	33	46	.08	Sunny	31	55	Cloudy	32	32
Cincinnati	45	50	.13	Sunny	38	51	Cloudy	38	55
Cleveland	36	41	.22	Sunny	36	48	Ptcldy	36	52
Columbia Sc	31	62	.00	Ptcldy	39	68	Sunny	40	72
Columbus Oh	39	44	.38	Sunny	37	50	Ptcldy	37	54
Dal Ft Worth	43	71	.00	Sunny	47	72	Cloudy	54	69
Denver	23	63	.00	Snoshw	30	50	Ptcldy	20	40
Des Moines	29	45	.00	Ptcldy	32	57	Cloudy	19	28
Detroit	30	46	.12	Sunny	33	46	Cloudy	32	42
Duluth	30	34	.00	Cloudy	30	37	Sunny	06	15
El Paso	31	66	.00	Ptcldy	33	70	Ptcldy	37	69
Fargo	23	37	.00	Windy	26	28	Ptcldy	01	21
Flagstaff	19	18	.00	Snow	30	39	Ptcldy	20	47
Great Falls	42	53	.00	Snoshw	10	32	Windy	20	46

FORECAST FOR THE REGION

New Mexico — Variable clouds Tuesday and Tuesday night, chance of showers and mountain snow showers mainly west and north. Highs Tuesday, 40 to 50 mountains and northwest. 50s to mid-70s lower elevations. Lows, teens to 20s mountains, mid-20s to near 40 lower elevations.

Kansas — Partly cloudy and mild Tuesday. Mostly cloudy Tuesday night, chance of light snow northwest and north-central. Highs Tuesday, mid-50s to mid-60s statewide, lows low 20s northwest, mid-30s east.

Utah — Mostly cloudy north Tuesday, scattered rain and snow showers, variable clouds south both days, widely scattered showers. Locally gusty winds statewide Tuesday. Highs Tuesday, mid-30s to mid-40s north, 40s south. Lows, low 20s-low 30s north, low 20s to mid-30s south.

Nebraska — Considerable clouds and colder Tuesday, increasing winds in afternoon, slight chance of showers west and north.

FOREIGN CITIES

City	Hi	Lo	Wth	City	Hi	Lo	Wth
				London	48	41	clr
				Madrid	57	43	clr
Acapulco	90	75	cdy	Mazatlan	87	71	cdy
Amsterdam	50	46	clr	Manila	88	66	clr
Athens	63	41	clr	Merida/Cancun	84	57	clr
Barbados	84	72	clr	Mexico City	73	46	clr
Berlin	45	37	cdy	Montreal	39	32	cdy
B'Aires	77	61	cdy	Moscow	36	34	sn
Cairo	66	48	clr	New Delhi	81	52	clr
Calgary	39	18	cdy	Ottawa	34	1	cdy
Copenhagen	49	41	clr	Paris	48	45	clr
Dublin	52	39	clr	Regina	24	−4	cdy
Edmonton	32	0	clr	Rome	55	34	clr
Frankfurt	46	32	cdy	San Juan	72	70	cdy
Geneva	39	32	cdy	Stockholm	45	37	clr
Guadalajara	80	41	clr	Tokyo	57	43	cdy
Hong Kong	73	64	clr	Toronto	39	32	cdy
Jerusalem	54	39	cdy	Vancouver	43	36	rn
Kingston	90	73	cdy	Vienna	39	32	cdy

Some newspapers also include information about the condition of local highways. Travelers can use this information to plan their routes.

In addition, the weather section reports on precipitation, air quality, humidity, and hourly temperatures for cities throughout the state. And if you are interested in knowing the temperature in Tokyo, you can consult the detailed, alphabetized lists of temperatures in cities throughout the world. The National Weather Service compiles these lists for various major cities around the globe.

Consult the charts in Figure 4.5 and you will see that Brownsville, Texas, and Barbados both had temperatures of 84 degrees on December 12, although one city had partly cloudy skies, while the other had clear skies. Now, try doing some more weather research on your own. Use the charts in Figures 4.2–4.5 to answer the following questions. Write your answers on a separate sheet of paper.

1. What is the expected high temperature on Tuesday in the New Mexico mountains?
2. What is the expected low temperature on Tuesday in the northwest section of Kansas?
3. What was Monday's low temperature in Albany?
4. What was Monday's high temperature in Dallas/Fort Worth?
5. How much precipitation was recorded in Detroit on Monday?
6. Which two cities on the national chart recorded the lowest temperature on Monday? What was the temperature?
7. Which city on the national chart recorded the highest temperature on Monday? What was the temperature?
8. Which two cities on the foreign chart recorded the highest temperature? What was the temperature?
9. What kind of weather is predicted for Denver?
10. What was the record low for Denver on December 11th? (Hint: It was set in 1932.)

ACTIVITY 4.12

Understanding Stock Quotations

Read the business section in your newspaper and you can learn about the stock market. Why is stock market activity such important news? Because the buying and selling that happens on Wall Street affects many individuals' incomes, as well as the economies of the United States and the world. Perhaps you have invested in stocks yourself. If so, you probably turn quickly to the stock quotations whenever you pick up a newspaper.

If you do not yet know how to read stock quotations, you are about to enter the world of Wall Street. To read and understand the stock exchange pages found in the business sections of all metropolitan papers, you must first learn some essential terms. On a separate sheet of paper, take notes on these terms and their definitions.

Year's high: the highest price the stock reached in one year's time.

Year's low: the lowest price the stock reached in one year's time.

Day's high: the highest price the stock reached on a given day.

Day's low: the lowest price the stock reached on a given day.

Last price: the price at which the stock was selling when the market closed for the day.

Net change: the difference between a stock's last price today and the same stock's last price on the previous day of trading.

NYSE: New York Stock Exchange: one of the major stock exchanges.

$7/8$ = 87.5 cents

$3/4$ = 75.0 cents

$5/8$ = 62.5 cents

$1/2$ = 50.0 cents

⅜ = 37.5 cents

¼ = 25.0 cents

⅛ = 12.5 cents

Now, look at the stock quotations that follow and answer questions one to four. Use the terminology you just learned to find the answers.

52-week High	Low	Stock	Div.	Yld.	PE	100s	Sales High	Low	Last	Chg.
$32^{1}/_{2}$	$21^{5}/_{8}$	Mattels					$27^{1}/_{4}$	$26^{5}/_{8}$	27	$-^{3}/_{8}$
53	$41^{1}/_{2}$	Goodyr					53	$51^{7}/_{8}$	$52^{7}/_{8}$	+1
$36^{3}/_{8}$	$25^{5}/_{8}$	Chryslrs					$35^{5}/_{8}$	$35^{1}/_{4}$	$35^{3}/_{8}$	...

1. What were the year's high, year's low, day's high, day's low, last price, and net change for Chrysler stock?

2. Using the stock quotations for Goodyear, provide the same information requested in Question 1.

3. Using the stock quotations for Mattel, provide the same information requested in Question 1.

4. Finally, survey the stock quotations for several companies whose names are familiar to you. Using a metropolitan newspaper, look up the year's high, year's low, day's high, day's low, last price, and net change for the following stocks: Alcoa, Campbell's Soup, Delta Air Lines, Exxon, and K-Mart.

Stock Quotation Worksheet

Are you a Wall Street wizard? Using the New York Stock Exchange (NYSE) quotations from a metropolitan paper, look up the following stocks and, on a separate sheet of paper, record these statistics for each stock listed below: the abbreviation for the stock, year's high, year's low, day's high, day's low, last price, and net change.

Ford Motor Company	Kellogg's	Texas Instruments
General Electric	Penney's	United Air Lines
Honda	PepsiCo	Wendy's
Motorola	Kimberley Clark	Xerox

After you find all the information requested above, answer, the following questions:

1. Which of the stocks has the highest *last* price per share?

2. What was that stock's *last* price?

3. Which of the stocks has the lowest *last* price per share?

4. What was that stock's *last* price?

5. Which stock recorded the largest *net gain* from the previous day?

6. How much did that stock gain?

7. Which stock recorded the largest *net loss* from the previous day?

8. How much was that stock down?

9. If you were buying one of these twelve stocks, which would you buy? Why?

ACTIVITY 4.14   ## Magazine Preferences

Reading for pleasure certainly must include magazines. You probably enjoy browsing through a favorite magazine relating to a hobby or a sport or cars or fashion. Some magazines are funny or inspirational; some magazines are interesting and informative. No matter what your reason for reading a specific magazine, you need to recognize that reading magazines is an important part of reading for pleasure.

And reading for enjoyment is important for developing reading speed, reading comprehension, and vocabulary. The more you read, the more practice you have improving your reading skills, the more contact you have with words and word meanings, and the more your reading speed improves. Although reading a magazine may seem like nothing but pure enjoyment, you benefit by doing it.

Let's begin by surveying your magazine reading habits. On a separate sheet of paper, number from one to five, skipping every other line. Answer the following questions regarding your leisure reading preferences.

1. Which magazine(s) do you enjoy reading most? Why?

2. Do you read the entire magazine, or do you read only parts of it? If you read only parts of it, which parts do you read?

3. Do you read entire articles in the magazine, or do you simply skim them? Why?

4. Where and when do you read magazines? Why do you choose this time and location?

5. Do you enjoy reading magazines more than reading books? Why?

ACTIVITY 4.15   ## Magazine Survey

There are hundreds of magazines on newsstands and library shelves today. Select a magazine you have never read before and skim through it. Choose an article that catches your interest or makes you curious and read it. Next using a separate sheet of paper, write down the name of the magazines you selected and the title of the article you read. Then briefly state the article's main idea. Do the same survey with a second magazine and, if you have time, a third magazine as well. (Remember, don't be tempted by your usual favorites—choose a magazine that's new to explore.) Be prepared to explain why you selected the magazines you did and to discuss whether you would like to continue to read those titles.

Magazine Summary

Bring to class a magazine you enjoy reading. Choose an article and, simply for pleasure, read it. Now, on a separate sheet of paper, write a short paragraph summarizing the gist of the article.

Was reading and summarizing easy or difficult for you? If it was easy, you are comprehending well enough during leisure reading to get the main idea of the content. Did you find yourself skimming the article, selectively skipping sentences or sections you did not enjoy, or did you read the article word for word? Were you still able to get the gist of the article using the skimming and skipping reading technique?

You do not have to feel guilty skimming and selectively skipping passages as you read for pleasure. After all, you are not reading for specific details; you are not going to be tested on the material. Reading for pleasure in your leisure time should be enjoyable!

Repeat this activity frequently. On a separate sheet of paper prepare a chart similar to the one shown. Each time you complete the exercise, log it on your chart.

Name of magazine	Title of article	Summary
1.		
2.		

Selecting an Enjoyable Book

Have you read any good books lately? For some people, sitting back and getting lost in a book is the most relaxing thing they can do.

Rediscover the joy of reading a book for pleasure. Your instructor will set aside some class time for leisure reading. Your task is to choose a book to read that you will enjoy. If you start a book and don't like it, select another. It defeats the purpose of this activity to have you suffer through a book you don't like.

The first step, then, is to find a book you will enjoy. You might ask your librarian to suggest some books other students have liked. Or, your instructor may have some ideas that interest you. On the other hand, you may prefer to browse independently, skimming covers and summaries to find a book that suits you. However you go about finding your books, enjoy this opportunity to get reacquainted with reading for pleasure.

Reading for Pleasure

Keep a record of your reading progress by making a chart like the one that follows. Each time you read your book, log on your chart the date and the number of pages you read.

Remember, as you read, your reading speed is increasing, your comprehension is improving, and your vocabulary is growing. Not bad, since reading a book you enjoy is a pleasure, anyway!

	Date	Number of pages read		Date	Number of pages read
1			4		
2			5		
3			6		

ACTIVITY 4.19

Creative Book Projects[1]

If your instructor says *book report*, she or he is likely to hear a loud groan in response. This activity gives you the opportunity to do something much more creative and fun than writing a typical book report. From the list that follows, choose the format for a creative book project that appeals to you. Be sure to include your book's title and author somewhere in your project.

1. Create a crossword puzzle based on you book. Include at least forty *Across* clues and forty *Down* clues and make certain that most of your clues are related directly to your book. The only exceptions to this rule are words or definitions that you have to use as "fillers." Include a key for the crossword puzzle.

2. Construct an exam of at least fifty questions based on your book. Include multiple-choice, matching, true-false, and completion questions on your exam. Try to use approximately the same number of each type of question. You may include other kinds of questions, such as short essays, but provide an outline of possible essay answers along with an answer key for the objective questions.

3. Design an oversized poster based on your book. Include in the design a 300-word recommendation "advertising" the book. This format lends itself very well to sports stories and mysteries.

4. Draw a detailed map of the book's primary setting and then explain in sequence the important action that occurred at the various places illustrated on your map. Completeness, creativity, and neatness are important here.

5. Choose either a major or minor character from your book and explain his or her part in the plot or sequence of events. Then, explain how you would have reacted or behaved differently.

6. You are a literary critic. Choose one of the following and discuss the statement, reflecting and amplifying on your book.

   A. "Authors are people behind masks."

   B. "The biographer is a maker of heels or heroes."

   C. "Show me what the age is reading, and I can tell you the nature of the times."

---

[1]The suggestions in this activity are taken from Isabelle M. Decker, *100 Novel Ways with Book Reports*. New York: Scholastic Magazines, Inc., 1969.

    D. "This book should be included in a capsule buried today, to be dug up in 100 years."

    E. "This book should be read by every young adult and his or her parents."

7. Condense the action in your book into various articles and present them as though they made up the front page of a newspaper. Use a standard six-column newspaper format. Include human interest stories, sports events, obituaries, editorials, want ads, advertising, and so on. Make sure all of your articles reflect the book you read and the era in which its story action took place. (For example, Tom Sawyer would not be riding a mountain bike.)

8. Write a television commercial about your book. Include all necessary dialogue, as well as descriptions of the story action. Draw pictures or use magazine illustrations to convey your ideas. The illustrations should reveal what your commercial would look like if shown on television.

9. If you choose to read a collection of short stories, you may wish to do one of the following:

    A. Write your intellectual reactions to five stories, rather than analyzing them. Discuss the type of reader who would enjoy or find satisfaction in reading each story. To justify your position, present at least three positive aspects of a story you like and three negative aspects of one you disliked.

    B. Write an essay on the significance and importance of titles, referring to the titles of ten specific stories to support your generalizations.

Traditional Book Projects

ACTIVITY 4.20

Some students feel more confident following a more conventional form for a book project, and some books lend themselves to this type of report format. If you are one of this group, or if you feel that the book you chose fits the traditional project category, try the following:

1. In the center of the page on a separate sheet of paper, write the title of the book you read and underline it. Beneath the title, write the author's name.

2. For Part One of your report, begin by describing the action in the book. In other words, what was the plot of the story?

Choose three of the following to conclude your book project.

3. Describe in detail the main character of the book you read. Include a description of his or her appearance, personality, motivations, and so on. Point out whether this character changed though the course of the story.

4. Describe what you consider the climax of the plot and tell why.

5. Discuss whether you think the book is true to life and, if not, why not.

6. Tell about the incident or aspect of the book that you either really liked or really disliked.

7. Give your general evaluation of the book, including what you liked and dislike about it. Would you recommend it to anyone else?

Review

Unit 4

Number a separate sheet of paper from one through twenty-five. Read the following questions and write the correct answers beside the corresponding numbers on your answer sheet.

I. Sections of the Newspaper (1–7)

Identify the section of the newspaper being described by writing the name of the section in the corresponding space on your answer sheet.

1. The _____ section deals with entertainment. It includes information about movies, plays, concerts, and nightlife. It also includes the comics.

2. This section is essential for the paper because it provides the money to publish the paper. It is called the _____ section.

3. The _____ is what the reader sees first. It influences his or her decision about whether to buy the paper.

4. _____ focus on individuals who have died and give accounts of occupation, relatives, funeral information, and so on.

5. The _____ section focuses on opinions of staff writers, the general public, and syndicated columnists.

6. The previous night's basketball game, the top sports statistics, and news of a player trade are covered in the _____ section.

7. Stock quotations are found in the _____ section, along with articles on new products, marketing strategies, and companies of note.

II. Newspaper Jargon (8–16)

Match the terms given with their correct definitions.

8. Banner headline
9. Headline
10. Byline
11. News agency
12. A.P.
13. Dateline
14. Lead
15. Caption
16. Jump

A. Continued on page _____.
B. The first paragraph of a story
C. Associated Press
D. The line indicating who wrote the article
E. Words beside or below a photograph or illustration
F. The line indicating when the described event took place
G. An organization that sends news stories by wire
H. Large type above and article indicating the content of the article
I. A headline that stretches from one side of the newspaper page to the other

III. Business and Financial Section (17–23)

Study the stock quotation given below and identify each numbered section with the term that describes it.

17.	18.	19.	20.	21.	22.	23.
13⅞	4⅞	Mattel	11½	11¼	11½	−¼

IV. Classified Ads (24)

Since you pay for Classified Ads by the word, it is your advantage to use as few words in an ad as possible. Rewrite the following classified ad, making it brief, yet complete. (Hint: thirty-five to forty words will supply all the necessary information.)

24. FOR SALE—I would like to sell for $75 the Victorian sofa my husband says is like new. I also have a dining room table and four chairs for $160 that I really want to get rid of. Because we have a new color TV set, I will also sell my 7-year-old portable TV for $24. Last year we bought a new G.E. Electric range for $750, but I really don't like it. I will be willing to let it go for $300. Anyone who is interested in any of these terrific bargains should call me at 123-4567. Be sure not to call until after 5:00 P.M. because I won't be home from work until then.

V. Reading for Pleasure (25)

No matter what you prefer to read—newspapers, magazines, or books—reading for pleasure is good for you.

25. In a short essay explain the benefits of reading for pleasure.

Answers are provided for most activities in this book. Answers are not provided for activities with open-ended questions or for activities that require personal responses.

UNIT 1

Improving Your Understanding

ACTIVITY 1.1

1. You report principal's office immediately take books
2. tryouts play Thursday 8:00 P.M. Room 208
3. flood destroyed homes bridges roads
4. Fourth of July special United States celebrates independence
5. Many states wide temperature changes four seasons
6. Susan Smith Joan Vickers president class Joan won
7. football championship tie North South High Schools
8. Peer pressure problem preteens teens
9. Regular attendance school important grades
10. Concentration required identify key words

ACTIVITY 1.2

Paragraph One: Teens are faced with many choices today. (first sentence)
Paragraph Two: Does weather affect you? (middle of paragraph)
Paragraph Three: Schools serve a variety of needs. (last sentence)
Paragraph Four: Students have many opportunities to become a part of a group and to acquire a sense of belonging. There are many ways to get involved. (first and last sentences)
Paragraph Five: Not stated
Paragraph Six: By now you know several things about the main idea of a paragraph. (first sentence)

ACTIVITY 1.3

Main Ideas:
1. Credit is a tool. (paragraph 1)
2. Credit has advantages and disadvantages. (paragraph 3)

Supporting Details:
Advantages of Credit Use
1. enables young people to make large purchases (e.g., furniture)
2. can use purchase before owning (e.g., car)
3. provides emergency funds
4. can purchase investments (e.g., home)

5. provides enjoyment of conveniences now
6. eliminates the need to carry sums of cash
7. credit payments may be a form of forced savings

Disadvantages of Credit Use
1. encourages overspending
2. makes it too easy to accumulate debt
3. incurs interest charges

ACTIVITY 1.4

1. **groceries**	2. **reactions**	3. **band awards**
apples	entered room	Spirit Award
flour	stopped	John Phillip Sousa Award
salt	mouth wide open	
sugar	eyes rounded in horror	

4. **scholarships**	5. **supplies**
Columbine Honor Society	backpack
Elks	pens
Altrusa	pencils
Frank-McKee Memorial	paper
Lions' Club	spiral notebooks
Music Teachers	eraser
Rotary Club International	highlighter

ACTIVITY 1.5

How to Scramble Eggs

Break eggs into bowl. Add 1 tablespoon milk or cream and a dash of salt and pepper for each egg. Beat well with a fork. Heat ½ tablespoon fat for each egg in moderately hot skillet. Pour in mixture and reduce heat to low. Cook slowly, turning gently as mixture sets at bottom and sides of pan. Avoid constant stirring. When cooked through but still moist (5 to 8 minutes), serve at once.

ACTIVITY 1.6

1. **Before**

Dress:	appropriate; commonly accepted for that profession; ask if not sure
Preparation:	go alone; arrive 5 to 10 minutes early; know what company makes or services it provides
Materials:	social security card; copies of résumé; names, addresses, phone numbers for references from three people not related to you; driver's license
References:	people employer can call about applicant

2. **During**

Present self:	polite; don't smoke or chew gum; look alert; make frequent eye contact; listen intently; answer questions clearly and completely; speak audibly; ask questions
Benefits:	ask only after offered job
Want job:	say so confidently

3. **After**

Follow-up:	thank interviewer; write thank-you note
Not contacted:	make return visit or call

ACTIVITY 1.7

Beginning	During	End
enthusiastic	confused—orders	discouraged—discussion
confident	tired—feet	positive—challenges
positive	clumsy—coke	organized—tip
	irritable—customers	service—tip
	impatient—babies	self-confidence—experience
	tired—feet	cheerful—smile
	frustrated—littered tables	
	discouraged—sticky plates	
	tired—feet	
	discouraged—small tips	

ACTIVITY 1.8

Answers will vary considerably, but may resemble the following:
1. younger child dressed in her Sunday best
2. tightwad
3. large older man with dominating personality, a bit dramatic
4. person with tremendous mood swings; doesn't hesitate to express opinions, but opinions are not consistent
5. beautiful young girl, beautiful teeth, long hair, fashion model

ACTITIVY 1.9

Answers will vary.
1. The description of Brahms as a publicly crusty bachelor and an outwardly eccentric man with an unimpressive appearance probably contributed to the reasons for his not marrying.
2. He was a talented man even as a teen, but was very unusual and perhaps not too endearing. The qualities mentioned in the previous response are not especially attractive qualities, and Brahms was probably a difficult man to know and like.

ACTIVITY 1.10

Paragraph One
1. bait
2. They probably will not catch any fish.
3. They have no bait.

Paragraph Two
1. He will be angry or disappointed with her.
2. her selfishness; the fact that she spent part of the money on herself
3. She may pretend to be delighted, but she will probably be disappointed. (Answers will vary but should be supported by the text.)
4. the fact that she did not get the necklace (Answers will vary.)
5. She will probably regret her purchase and feel guilty.

Paragraph Three

1. fire Sean
2. Sean has been late twice; his boss has warned him; his boss is collecting carts, which is Sean's job.
3. Yes, because despite the number of times he was late, the number of warnings, and the fact that his boss was patient, Sean did not change.

ACTIVITY 1.11

1. You must adjust to the speed of the speaker.
2. You cannot choose the time and place for listening.
3. Once something is spoken, it is gone.
4. Critical thinking and listening are difficult to do simultaneously.
5. Distractions are hard to ignore.
6. Personal prejudices may bias you.
7. The reactions of others may influence your listening skills.

Effect on grades: Answers will vary, but should indicate that poor listening skills may mean poor grades.

ACTIVITY 1.12

Answers will vary.

1. It might rain.
2. The referee made an unpopular call; the home team probably lost.
3. The weather is lousy; it is winter; they will probably stay indoors.
4. It was a bird that was unknown to them.
5. Christmas is near—perhaps it's the night before Christmas.
6. They were participating in a game show and the spin of the wheel was about to decide the outcome.
7. A football game is being described and it is time for the kickoff.
8. The student probably received a poor or failing grade.
9. The students are probably in chemistry lab, and they caused an explosion.
10. Jana won the election.

ACTIVITY 1.13

1. was	9. was	17. had	25. at
2. hill	10. prickles	18. stage	26. crept
3. moon	11. you	19. shadows	27. I
4. the	12. the	20. or	28. feet
5. was	13. imaginations	21. tried	29. popped
6. first	14. does	22. five	30. not
7. enough	15. trails	23. a	31. and
8. fresh	16. especially	24. imaginary	32. mountainside

UNIT 1 REVIEW

I. Completion

1. main idea	3. sequencing	5. Cloze
2. Comprehension	4. cause	

II.   **Short Essay**

IIA.   There are several things you can do to become a better student.... As you can see, there are many things you can do to become a better student.

IIB.   1. Create a good study setting.
2. Budget your time.
3. Improve your note-taking abilities.
4. Develop and use good test-taking skills.
5. Understand the value of reading different material at appropriate and vastly different rates.
6. Develop your listening skills.

III. Application

Answers will vary.

IV. Cloze

1. are
2. your
3. last
4. employer
5. of
6. search
7. as
8. sight

9. for
10. lower
11. take
12. pays
13. time
14. search
15. find
16. project

17. should
18. search
19. in
20. or
21. time
22. the
23. for
24. of

UNIT 2   # Increasing Speed

ACTIVITY 2.1

1. 4 (side)
2. 5 (card)
3. 2 (mail)
4. 3 (naps)
5. 5 (bore)
6. 1 (raid)
7. 3 (book)

8. 1 (cake)
9. 2 (tear)
10. 4 (took)
11. 5 (melt)
12. 3 (tape)
13. 1 (jack)
14. 4 (veal)

15. 2 (rats)
16. 5 (pump)
17. 3 (dale)
18. 4 (poor)
19. 1 (tool)
20. 2 (part)

ACTIVITY 2.2

1. 4 (dull)
2. 4 (desk)
3. 2 (last)
4. 3 (mask)
5. 5 (made)
6. 4 (rail)
7. 1 (hook)

8. 2 (rule)
9. 5 (hope)
10. 1 (took)
11. 4 (bone)
12. 5 (clad)
13. 3 (dirt)
14. 4 (feel)

15. 2 (boat)
16. 3 (jeer)
17. 1 (pony)
18. 4 (real)
19. 5 (pare)
20. 1 (belt)

ACTIVITY 2.3

1. 2 (scene)
2. 3 (active)

8. 4 (closed)
9. 1 (rough edge)

15. 3 (dressed)
16. 2 (question)

3. 2 (depend)
4. 3 (stop short)
5. 3 (warm oneself)
6. 2 (promises)
7. 1 (hint)

10. 2 (slight sign)
11. 4 (grow)
12. 2 (skillful act)
13. 2 (easy talk)
14. 1 (cook)

17. 3 (short breath)
18. 2 (smell)
19. 3 (bridle strap)
20. 2 (who inherits)

ACTIVITY 2.4

1. 1 (blurt)
2. 3 (flour)
3. 2 (metal)
4. 4 (alien)
5. 5 (cheek)
6. 2 (curly)
7. 1 (abide)

8. 5 (blood)
9. 4 (chunk)
10. 3 (blush)
11. 1 (glaze)
12. 5 (wrist)
13. 3 (floor)
14. 4 (shape)

15. 2 (width)
16. 3 (crazy)
17. 1 (blush)
18. 4 (medal)
19. 2 (chute)
20. 5 (share)

ACTIVITY 2.5

1. 2 (bonus)
2. 5 (shame)
3. 3 (write)
4. 1 (weight)
5. 4 (glass)
6. 1 (blunt)
7. 2 (dingy)

8. 3 (wield)
9. 5 (gland)
10. 4 (wrist)
11. 2 (block)
12. 4 (false)
13. 1 (boils)
14. 3 (aides)

15. 5 (chase)
16. 1 (legal)
17. 2 (rebel)
18. 3 (champ)
19. 3 (agent)
20. 4 (brief)

ACTIVITY 2.6

1. 1 (of voice)
2. 1 (slow talk)
3. 3 (evade)
4. 4 (display)
5. 2 (odor)
6. 1 (very thin)
7. 2 (to modify)

8. 2 (test)
9. 2 (kingdom)
10. 2 (pain)
11. 1 (entertain)
12. 4 (change)
13. 3 (pointed end)
14. 4 (servant)

15. 1 (dwelling)
16. 4 (entry hall)
17. 1 (swarm)
18. 3 (of sun)
19. 4 (hold and use)
20. 3 (alive)

ACTIVITY 2.7

1. 2 (belief)
2. 4 (censor)
3. 3 (facial)
4. 1 (agency)
5. 5 (devise)
6. 2 (hinder)
7. 4 (likely)

8. 1 (pardon)
9. 3 (racket)
10. 5 (ripple)
11. 1 (shrewd)
12. 3 (thrash)
13. 2 (recoil)
14. 3 (serial)

15. 4 (reflex)
16. 1 (snatch)
17. 5 (static)
18. 2 (gravel)
19. 3 (hooves)
20. 4 (mingle)

ACTIVITY 2.8

1. 3 (modify)
2. 5 (nibble)
3. 1 (pellet)
4. 4 (rescue)
5. 2 (sadden)
6. 4 (spider)
7. 1 (broken)

8. 3 (change)
9. 5 (commit)
10. 2 (damper)
11. 2 (gamble)
12. 4 (indent)
13. 1 (jangle)
14. 3 (misuse)

15. 5 (oppose)
16. 2 (radial)
17. 4 (seaman)
18. 1 (hubbub)
19. 3 (limber)
20. 5 (memory)

ACTIVITY 2.9

1.	4 (simple)	8.	4 (smear)
2.	3 (very busy)	9.	2 (stroke)
3.	3 (heavy rain)	10.	4 (brave)
4.	4 (enjoy)	11.	2 (shaking)
5.	3 (fault)	12.	4 (bad smell)
6.	1 (hot and humid)	13.	2 (be unlike)
7.	1 (soften)	14.	4 (royal law)

15. 2 (great dislike)
16. 2 (give)
17. 4 (make angry)
18. 3 (state meaning)
19. 2 (come out)
20. 1 (bring about)

ACTIVITY 2.10

1.	1 (baggage)	8.	3 (invalid)
2.	3 (calcium)	9.	5 (justice)
3.	2 (dolphin)	10.	4 (kindred)
4.	5 (flatten)	11.	2 (larceny)
5.	4 (gratify)	12.	1 (martial)
6.	2 (hemlock)	13.	3 (nitrate)
7.	1 (illegal)	14.	5 (officer)

15. 4 (plaster)
16. 4 (rampant)
17. 2 (rectify)
18. 1 (secular)
19. 3 (sparkle)
20. 5 (timeout)

ACTIVITY 2.12

1. False	3. False	5. False	7. True	9. False
2. True	4. True	6. False	8. True	10. True

ACTIVITY 2.13

1. True	3. False	5. False	7. False	9. False
2. True	4. True	6. False	8. False	10. False

ACTIVITY 2.14

1. True	3. True	5. True	7. False	9. True
2. False	4. False	6. False	8. True	10. False

ACTIVITY 2.15

1. False	3. True	5. False	7. False	9. True
2. True	4. True	6. False	8. True	10. False

UNIT 2 REVIEW

I. True-False

1. False	3. True	5. True	7. True	9. False
2. False	4. True	6. False	8. True	10. False

II. Multiple-Choice

11. D. A, B, and C
12. A. one

13. C. two or more
14. C. 2.5 to 3

III. Matching

15–16. C. Chew gum as you read.
        E. Hold a pencil clenched between your teeth.

17–18.   D.   Talk about the problem to yourself.
          F.   Read rapidly under timed conditions.
19–20.   B.   Place your hand against the side of your head.
          G.   Hold your chin firmly in your hand.
21.   A.   Fold your hands and let your eyes do the work.

IV. Short Essay

22.   **Value:** Drills help students increase the number of letters and words they can see per fixation; help them see letters and words more quickly; and help them discriminate between letters, words, and meanings with split-second accuracy, thus improving their reading speeds.
        Helpfulness: Answers will vary.

23.   Answers could include the following:
- Reading speed is personal and varies from one person to the next.
- Reading speed is flexible.
- Reading speed is determined by the purpose for reading, the difficulty of the material, and the reader's background.
- Increased reading speed without proper comprehension is useless.
- Building reading speed takes desire, determination, effort, self-discipline, and practice.
- Bad reading habits slow readers down.
- A good vocabulary improves reading speed.

        Application: Answers will vary.

Skimming and Scanning

UNIT 3

ACTIVITY 3.1

1.   A.   purpose;
    B.   degree of difficulty of material;
    C.   familiarity of material.
2.   A.   *Scanning* is glancing at materials until you find the information that you are looking for.
    B.   You should use scanning when you are seeking a particular fact or piece of information.
3.   A.   *Skimming* is passing over all the material to get an overview.
    B.   Skimming is used when you want to get a general idea of content.
4.   A.   Very rapid—light, entertaining reading.
    B.   Rapid—fairly easy material, when only the most important facts are needed.
    C.   Average—some studying, most everyday material.
    D.   Slow and careful—(from 50 to 250 wpm) for difficult concepts, for retaining every detail.
5.   A.   temperament
    B.   intelligence

ACTIVITY 3.2

Preview—looking quickly at the material *before* actual reading takes place;
Review—viewing the material *again* following a previous reading;
Overview—gaining an *overall* impression of content.

ACTIVITY 3.4

1. A. every class.
2. B. daily.
3. B. after your last class ends, but before you leave school.
4. C. both of the above
5. C. one and one-half hours of study time each night.
6. C. both of the above
7. B. they make it harder for you to complete the work and do it well.
8. C. both of the above
9. C. both of the above
10. C. every evening.

ACTIVITY 3.5

1. C. an orphan.
2. B. a milk bottle
3. B. preemies.
4. C. both A and B
5. A. a bathtub.
6. C. both A and B
7. A. Pincushion.
8. B. greed for food.
9. C. both A and B
10. A. cared very much for the lambs.

ACTIVITY 3.6

Answers will vary, but should include that the article centers around ten suggestions for dealing with one's boss and an explanation of each suggestion. Employees who follow the ten suggestions can look forward to good relationships with their bosses and success at their jobs.

ACTIVITY 3.7

Answers will vary, but should state that bosses are human and unique; each has his or her own style of management. An employee should analyze his or her boss's style and perform accordingly to be successful.

ACTIVITY 3.10

1. June 1, 1976
2. August 12, 1980
3. 7-02-82
4. 10/5/85
5. 6-21-86
6. March 17, 1987
7. January 25, 1989
8. 8-08-90
9. Nov. 4, 1990
10. September 5, 1991
11. May 1, 1992
12. 1/12/93
13. 2/14/94
14. 12/25/94
15. 4/25/95

ACTIVITY 3.11

1. 5:53
2. seven

3. Cary, Cumberland, Edison Park
4. twelve
5. 10:44, 640
6. six, Wendella Commuter Boat Service
7. one hour and eleven minutes, fifty-four minutes
8. 4:50 A.M. through 1:08 A.M.
9. six, 612
10. 622, 624

ACTIVITIES 3.12 AND 3.13

1. False	3. True	5. True	7. False	9. False
2. True	4. False	6. False	8. True	10. True

UNIT 3 REVIEW

I. Vocabulary Terms

1. review
2. skimming
3. preview
4. slow and careful reading
5. very rapid
6. scanning
7. overview
8. average
9. rapid

II. Completion

10–12. purpose, difficulty, and background
13–14. temperament and intelligence
15–18. • look at the title, author, and publication date;
   • look at the table of contents;
   • read the preface or introduction;
   • leaf through the rest of the material, looking at headings, charts, pictures, graphs, and so on.

III. Application

19. slow and careful
20. average or rapid
21. scanning
22. scanning
23. rapid or very rapid
24. slow and careful
25. average or rapid

Reading for Enjoyment

UNIT 4

ACTIVITY 4.10

1. Atlantic Division and Central Division
2. Midwest Division and Pacific Division

3. Atlantic Division—Miami   Central Division—Chicago
   Midwest Division—Houston   Pacific Division—L.A. Lakers
4. All have lost 21 games.
5. Atlantic Division—Boston   Midwest Division—Vancouver
   Central Division—Toronto   Pacific Division—Phoenix
6. Chicago   28 wins   4 losses   .875 pct.   18–3 in conference play
7. Toronto   10 wins   21 losses   .323 pct.

ACTIVITY 4.11

1. 40 to 50 degrees
2. lows 20s
3. 22 degrees
4. 71 degrees
5. 0.12 inches
6. Bismarck and Flagstaff; 19 degrees
7. Brownsville; 82 degrees
8. Acapulco and Kingston; 90 degrees
9. cold air and snow showers (overcast skies and rain turning to snow)
10. –13 degrees

ACTIVITY 4.12

1. $32\frac{1}{2}$; $21\frac{5}{8}$; $27\frac{1}{4}$; $26\frac{5}{8}$; 27; $-\frac{3}{8}$.
2. 53; $41\frac{1}{2}$; 53; $51\frac{7}{8}$; $52\frac{7}{8}$; +1.
3. $36\frac{3}{8}$; $25\frac{5}{8}$; $35\frac{5}{8}$; $35\frac{1}{4}$; $35\frac{5}{8}$; . . .
4. Answers will vary with daily stock market trading results.

UNIT 4 REVIEW

I. Sections of the Newspaper

1. feature
2. advertising
3. front page
4. Obituaries
5. editorial
6. sports
7. business/financial

II. Newspaper Jargon

8. I
9. H
10. D
11. G
12. C
13. F
14. B
15. E
16. A

III. Business and Financial Section

17. year's high
18. year's low
19. name of stock
20. day's high
21. day's low
22. last price
23. net change

IV. Classified Ads

24. Victorian sofa, like new, $75; dining room table and four chairs, $160; 7-year-old portable TV, $24; 1-year-old G.E. electric range, new $750, now $300. Call 123–4567 after 5:00 P.M.

Reading for Pleasure

25. Though they will vary, answers should include increasing reading speed, reading comprehension, and vocabulary.